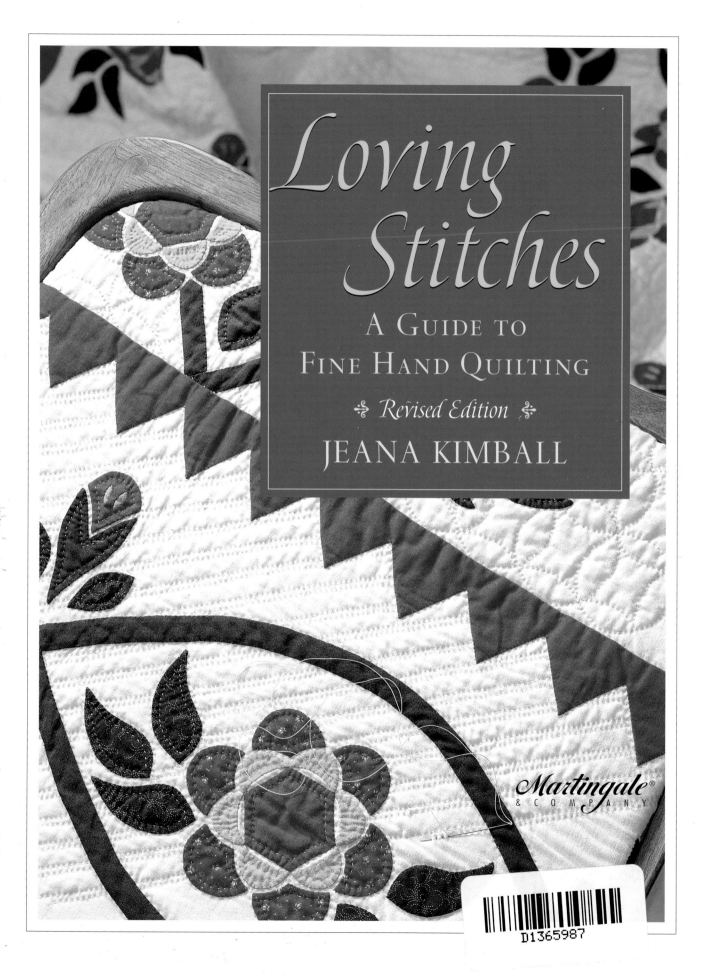

Loving Stitches

A GUIDE TO FINE HAND QUILTING

❖ Revised Edition ❖

JEANA KIMBALL

Martingale
& COMPANY

Credits

President ◆ *Nancy J. Martin*
CEO ◆ *Daniel J. Martin*
Publisher ◆ *Jane Hamada*
Editorial Director ◆ *Mary V. Green*
Managing Editor ◆ *Tina Cook*
Technical Editor ◆ *Jane Townswick*
Copy Editor ◆ *Liz McGehee*
Design Director ◆ *Stan Green*
Illustrator ◆ *Laurel Strand*
Cover and Text Designer ◆ *Trina Stahl*
Photographer ◆ *Brent Kane*

That Patchwork Place® is an imprint of Martingale & Company®.

Loving Stitches: A Guide to Fine Hand Quilting
Revised Edition
© 2003 by Jeana Kimball

Martingale & Company
20204 144th Avenue NE
Woodinville, WA 98072-8478 USA
www.martingale-pub.com

Printed in China
07 06 05 04 03   8 7 6 5 4 3 2 1

Library of Congress Cataloging-in-Publication Data

Kimball, Jeana.
    Loving stitches / Jeana Kimball.
        p. cm.
    ISBN 1-56477-498-8
    1. Quilting. I. Title.
    TT835.K4888 2003
    746.46—dc21   2003013858

Mission Statement

Dedicated to providing quality products and service to inspire creativity.

Dedication

To my mother, Loraine Hoyt Jones (1924–2000)

It was my mother's love of quilting that introduced me to quiltmaking. During the last years of her life, she patiently suffered through a terminal illness that first took her hands. In those five years, I only saw her exhibit frustration once—when she was unable to help me put a quilt on the frame.

Thank you, Mom.

Acknowledgments

Heartfelt thanks go to Charlotte Warr-Andersen, Marian Baker, Donna Eines, Eliza Gutke, Jeanne Huber, and Eleanor Tracy for the loan of their beautiful quilts to illustrate portions of this book. Judy Roche and Linda Gabrielse were especially generous in the loan of their valuable antique quilts to grace the pages of this book. I am very grateful for the willingness of all of these people to entrust their quilts to us for photography.

Additional thanks also goes to Stearns Technical Textiles Company (Mountain Mist Batting), Fairfield Processing, Quilters Dream Cotton, Ott-Lite Technology, StenSource International, Inc., and Sewing Notions, Inc. for donations of their products for research and photography.

I would especially like to thank Jim Bagley of The Grace Frame Company who generously donated several quilt frames for research and photography.

And, finally, I am most appreciative to Jane Townswick for her drive, clear thinking, and support through the process of reworking this book with me. She has been a great aid to this effort!

Contents

Preface

OVER TEN YEARS have passed since this book was first written. During that time, my experience and knowledge about the topic of hand quilting has increased. In this new era of a faster-paced life and machine-quilted quilts, I believe more firmly than ever that hand quilting is a valid and desirable finish to a quilt. The process is soothing, the work satisfying, and in the end, your quilt is undeniably a piece of you and your life during the weeks, months, or years it took to complete. I have an 80-year-old friend who built a business from scratch and made a great deal of money. She now spends her days writing her personal history because she wants her children and grandchildren to know her through her words, not by the money they will one day inherit. Our quilts are a stitched history of our lives that will reveal without words who we are and how we chose to spend our time. What a great legacy our hand-quilted quilts have the potential to become for our posterity!

Quilting—The Frosting on the Cake

THE DAY A quilt top was stretched on the quilting frame was always an exciting time for me as a small child. First, it meant all of the furniture in the living room was pushed back, making the room look large and impressive. Next, the long rails and stands were set up with the quilt stretched over them, making a perfect playhouse for me and my younger sisters. And, best of all, it meant that Grandma and some of the aunts would come by to "help with the quilting," sometimes for as many as three or four days in a row. What a treat it was to play with our dolls under the frame or quietly listen to the grown-up talk going on overhead! Occasionally, if we were very good, we could have a tea party under the quilt canopy.

As I grew older, I was glad quilting days came only once or twice each year. When I became a teenager, I was able and expected to help with the quilting or to take over daily household chores. My older sister wisely adapted to quilting at the frame with the ladies, but I had a more difficult time. Sitting in a straight-backed chair with one arm on top and one underneath the quilt was uncomfortable for me. But worst of all was never knowing when the next prick of the needle would come, whether it would draw blood, or worse yet, whether the prick would hurt. All this time, I was trying to keep a thimble on my middle finger and remember to use it once in a while. All in all, quilting made me fidget and wish I were someplace else. Fixing meals, washing dishes, and folding laundry were preferable to quilting back then. Years later, I learned that there is more than one way to stabilize the quilt "sandwich" while putting in quilting stitches to avoid the dreaded needle pricks. Now I prefer quilting over any household task!

Next best to the quilting is planning what to quilt. There is nothing like finishing a quilt top and standing back to take a look. It is time to savor and appreciate what you have done and look forward to the next process: quilting. Quilting adds a new dimension of texture and motion to the quilt, like adding the frosting to a cake.

Unfortunately, many quilters find it difficult to choose a quilting design. A debate begins within: How much is enough quilting? Are straight lines or curved ones better? Should I follow the outline of the pattern or impose a secondary design over the quilt surface? The debate goes on and on and sometimes the quilting never gets started, let alone finished!

The good news is there is no right or wrong way to quilt a quilt. You are the creator and can make up the rules as you go along. When my mother, grandmother, and aunts sat down to quilt a top, the decision was easy: Avoid the seams as much as possible, choose a quilting format that several people could easily work on at the same time, and select a design that could be completed in the shortest amount of time. You, too, will find that you have certain criteria for your quilting design.

The focus of this book is to help you recognize your own criteria, to point out considerations, traditions, and options, and to help you with your decision of how to quilt your top. There is also lots of information about quilting tools, patterns, and different ways to stitch. There is no need to procrastinate any longer—just get started!

Remember, "practice makes perfect." If you quilt a little bit every day, your stitches will improve, becoming smaller and easier to make. An added bonus is that your fingers will not be sore, because small calluses will form on the fingers that get the most pressure from the needle. I truly enjoy the rhythmic process of quilting every day and am often amazed at the volume of work that can be produced by spending only an hour or two each day stitching. Time spent hand quilting is never wasted. The stitches you take will always be there as tangible evidence of at least one thing you did each day. Aunt Jane of Kentucky, a fictional southern quilter from a book by Eliza Calvert Hall, expressed similar sentiments when she said, ". . . when I am dead and gone there ain't anybody goin' to think o' the floors I've swept, and the tables I've scrubbed, and the old clothes I've patched, and the stockin's I've darned. But when one o' my grandchildren or great-grandchildren sees one o' these quilts, they'll think about Aunt Jane, and, wherever I am then, I'll know I ain't forgotten."

Happy stitching!

"Hexagon Rose" by Jeana Kimball and
Loraine Hoyt Jones, 1990, Ivins, Utah, 78" x 76½".

A Brief History

*T*HE TRADITION OF stitching layers of fabric together for warmth—quilting—is believed to be so ancient that it may have preceded the written word. The British Museum owns a carved ivory figure of a pharaoh of the Egyptian First Dynasty, circa 3400 B.C. The figure is wearing a mantle or robe covered with a diamond pattern that suggests quilting.[1] However, the earliest surviving example of actual quilted goods is a carpet in the Leningrad Department of Institution of the Academy of Science of the USSR, dating from between 100 B.C. and 200 A.D. It was found being used as a floor covering in a tomb in northern Mongolia.[2]

Surviving evidence indicates that quilting was already a highly developed kind of needlework in the Middle East and Far East before it was introduced in European countries during the Crusades. Its first use in European countries was as quilted, coat-type garments for armor, to lessen the impact of weapons during battle. Later, similar quilted garments were worn under metal armor as padded protection against the metal suits. Little more is known about quilting until the sixteenth century, when written references indicate quilting's use in both clothing and bedding.

It has long been assumed that the function and popularity of quiltmaking began in humble peasant cottages in rural England as a practical way of providing

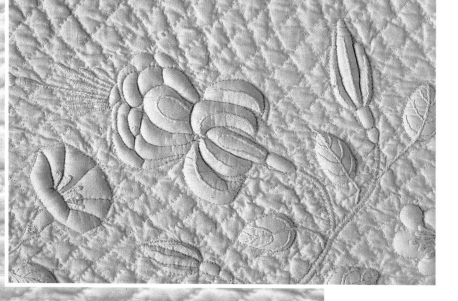

LEFT: *"Cradle Quilt" by Sarah Varick Hewlett, c. 1830, New York, 48" x 63". This remarkable cradle quilt features stuff work, embroidery detail, and stipple quilting, all done with 24 stitches per inch. Other areas on the quilt feature stuffed roses, ivy, birds, and butterflies. (Photo courtesy of DAR Museum, Washington, D.C., Acc. no. 87.43)*

Detail of border area on a whole-cloth quilt by Ann Pamela Cunningham, 1835–40, Rosemont Plantation, Laurens County, South Carolina, 97" x 104". Miss Cunningham made this extraordinary quilt prior to founding the Mount Vernon Ladies Association of the Union. Miss Cunningham was an invalid from the age of 18, when she was thrown from her horse. Note the two rows of interlocked hearts that define the border area of this quilt. (Photo courtesy of DAR Museum, Washington, D.C., Acc. no. 54.160)

warmth. However, in her book, *Traditional British Quilts,* Dorothy Osler points out that the opposite is true. The earliest bed quilts documented are of expensive materials. From *The Romance of Arthur of Lytel Brytayne,* there is mention of a "rich quilt wrought with coten, with crimson sendel (silk) stitched with thredes of gold." [3] There are numerous listings of fine quilts in estate inventories of the wealthy and noble classes in England in early centuries, but no mention of quilts in the property inventories of the lower classes.

Seventeenth-century estate records indicate more widespread ownership of linen quilts in all classes. Quilted bedding continued to grow in popularity in all economic classes and met its most popular use in the eighteenth century. The fashions of that century included elaborately quilted petticoats stitched from silk and satin and worn under dresses with cutaway skirts to expose the workmanship. This fashion was practiced universally throughout Britain, Europe, and the American colonies. The warmth and fullness supplied by a quilted underskirt was desirable long after fashion changed. "It was not uncommon for women to wear three or more petticoats. One quilted, or of flannel, one of alpaca or silk moiré, which rustled and swished, and one or several—white embroidery or lace-trimmed with frills . . . Dorfy, South Shields (1904–1914)." [4]

As the demand for quilted petticoats and bed coverings grew, both men and women took on quiltmaking as a profession. As early as 1563, there was a listing in the British Fugitive Trades for "Broyderers, Taylors, Quylters and Limners." [5] Professional quiltmakers

were employed most frequently in the eighteenth and nineteenth centuries. Quilt marker or stamper also became an established profession with apprentices and paid workers. Often, the professional marker first served as an apprentice to a tailor and had a natural artistic ability. Drawing a quilting pattern on material took from two to five days. [6] *Traditional British Quilts* describes how Elizabeth Sanderson, a well-known quilt marker in Northern England, took on her first quilt-marker apprentice:

> . . . she was the daughter of a farming butcher at the head of Weardale. On leaving school at the age of fourteen, in the 1890s, she set out one morning to walk the six miles over the fel to Allenheads, carrying her provisions for the week—bread, butter, sugar and so forth. She served for one year without payment. . . . She then became a paid hand, earning about four shillings a week and her board and lodging. [7]

In this country, there were professional quilt markers as well. A 1747 Boston paper announced: "Sarah Hunt, dwelling in the house of James Nichol in School Street, stamped Counterpins, curtains, linens and cottons for quilting with fidelity and Despatch." [8]

The most notorious professional quiltmaker in all of England was Joe Hedley, better known as "Joe the Quilter" or "the Hermit of Warden." Joe was born in the mid-1700s and trained as a tailor, but became most well known for his quilt designs and stitching. The story goes that his work was sent as far away as Ireland and America. His quilting was very fine—sometimes stitched at quarter-inch intervals, and he was partial to flowers, chains, and diamond shapes.[9] Joe was probably no more skilled than many other professional quilters, but his untimely death (an unsolved murder) made his quilts and story part of the local folklore. His life and death were memorialized in a 24-verse poem by A. Wright.

During the eighteenth and nineteenth centuries, it is said (possibly apocryphally) to have been customary for a young woman to make a "baker's dozen" (quilts) for her dower chest. The 13th quilt of this group was her masterpiece, designed to display her skill with a needle. Often this "best" quilt was an appliqué design, but some girls chose to stitch a whole-cloth counterpane. The counterpane's front was usually a fine white cotton. The backing was generally more coarsely woven, sometimes even hand-woven. Many needlework techniques, such as embroidery, candlewicking, and tufting, could be featured on the quilt's front, but the counterpane always included cording, stuff work, and lots of quilting. Often, the only filling between the layers was the cotton filler in the stuff-work motifs. With no batting between the layers, small, even stitches were easy to make, and the corded and stuff-work motifs stood out with extra dimension. The quilts on pages 7 and 46 are examples of white whole-cloth spreads. For more information on stuff work, also known as trapunto, see page 24.

Many layette quilts were also of the white counterpane type. In her book, *Old Patchwork Quilts and the Women Who Made Them*, Ruth Finley says, "the time came when no crib was complete without its snow-white quilt."[10] She then tells the story of an old woman from upstate New York and one of her unfinished crib quilts.

It seems that upon the death of the old woman, who was the sole resident of an old stone house in upstate New York, the townsfolk found her home filled with unusual items. "Old Maid Smith" as she was known locally had isolated herself from the community following the death of her parents while she was in her twenties. She spent her life sewing and reading. The postmaster said, "She subscribed to more magazines and papers than the County School Superintendent himself or even the Carnegie Library." Packed away in barrel-topped trunks they found "dozens of yellowed, unused garments—laces and silks and linens—the trousseau of a bride. And in a great chest-on-chest there was drawer after drawer filled to overflowing with infants' things, dainty layettes—not one, but enough for a whole family of babies." Among the baby things was an unfinished baby quilt with a beautiful feather border. A template for the unusually lacy feather plumes is found on page 61.[11]

Generally, whole-cloth quilted designs were reserved for best quilts in the United States, with many more patchwork quilts being made and used for everyday purposes. In England, whole-cloth quilts were used for everyday. Sometimes the quilt top was strip pieced, but lovely overall quilting was always featured. In other words, the quilting design became secondary on most American quilts, while it continued as a major element on British quilts.

Quilted petticoat, maker unknown, 1740–70, possibly made in England, waist 26½", and 36" long. This beautifully executed blue silk petticoat is backed with linen. Notice that the upper section of the petticoat is plainly quilted with a simple grid, but the lower edge, which might accidentally be seen, is closely quilted with an elaborate design featuring leaves and flowers. (Photo courtesy of DAR Museum, Washington, D.C., Acc. no. 78-48)

Planning Quilting Designs

WHEN PLANNING HOW you will quilt your top, do not underestimate the importance quilting plays in the overall visual impact of your quilt. At one quilt show I attended—as is often the case—one quilt received more attention than the others. The pieced design in that quilt was well done, but the quilting was extraordinary, the subject of many compliments. If the quilt had not been so finely quilted, it would not have been noticed by most visitors. You can make your quilts "show stoppers" by choosing quilting designs that enhance and add texture to the pieced or appliquéd designs of your quilt tops.

In general, when planning how far apart to place lines of quilting and what the scale of the quilting motifs should be, look to the proportions of the quilt top as a starting place. For example, a bed-size quilt with 12" pieced blocks is made up of larger-scale pieces than the same pattern done as a wall quilt with 6" blocks. The quilting lines on the larger quilt should be placed farther apart (1" to 2") in keeping with its overall scale. The wall quilt, because of its much smaller size, would warrant closer quilting (½" to ¾") to maintain its smaller scale. The same concept applies to the scale of feathers, cables, or any other designs you wish to incorporate as quilting patterns.

Quilting heavily in the center of a quilt and quilting sparsely on its borders will make the outside edges of the quilt wavy. Quilting stitches have a tendency to "draw up" a quilt, especially if it is being lap or hoop quilted. If a quilt is not consistently quilted with the same amount of quilting over the entire surface, the result will be bulging or wavy places that cannot be remedied.

For a patchwork top, the quilting should complement, not detract from, the lines of the piecing. Keep in mind that the quilting stitches and overall quilted design will stand out more on areas of solid-colored fabric than on pieced areas and printed fabrics. For example, the quilting in the center of a scrap quilt will not be nearly as evident as the quilting design on a plain border that surrounds it. The viewer's eye will follow the patchwork pattern over the patchwork surface, but when there is a plain area, the quilting design will stand out more, inviting the viewer to study it. Quilting designs on these plain areas must be carefully chosen to enhance the rest of the quilt top. Since many appliqué quilts have white or very light backgrounds, the quilting choices you make are as important as the appliqué itself. See "Understanding the Design Process" on page 30 for discussions of how I chose quilting formats and the scale for two of my quilts.

To help you decide how you want to quilt your quilt top, read through the following questions. As you consider each one, you will be able to refine your quilting design choices to complement each quilt you make.

♦ *What is the quilt's intended function?* A utility quilt needs only enough quilting to hold the layers together securely, and it is possible that a tied finish may be sufficient. Machine quilting is also an option. On the opposite end of the spectrum is a masterpiece quilt or a very best quilt. This type of quilt warrants lavish quilting, much more than is necessary to hold the layers together. The more quilted detail added, the better the "masterpiece" effect will be.

"When it comes to quilting, too much is not enough," is a quote I heard when I first started quilting. In studying old quilts over the years, I've come to agree; the ones I admire the most are usually very lavishly quilted. The next time you visit a quilt show, pay attention to the winners. I am sure you will find that they have much more quilting than is required to simply hold the layers together. If you plan to enter your quilts in competition, you will want to keep this in mind while you plan the quilting design and placement.

◆ *Is the quilt a gift?* Who will use it and how? A majority of the quilts being made today are given as gifts. If the quilt is for a child, remember that the quilt will probably be used and loved with little respect for the time you spent hand quilting. Therefore, do not put so much quilting into it that you will be offended or unhappy if the quilt is "used up" in a few years.

Will the recipient (and the recipient's family) appreciate, and take care of your gift? We have all heard horror stories of a lovely quilt gift being used as a dog bed, picnic blanket, or padding for moving furniture. Even though it sounds cold and calculating, consider how this quilt will be cared for in its new home.

◆ *How much time do you have to complete this quilt?* Do you have a required completion date? If so, the decision of how much quilting to use may already be made for you. Many of us work best, or at least faster, under pressure, but only so much is possible in a given time period. Don't start a quilting format that you will be unable to complete in the time allowed.

◆ *Will more than one person work on this quilt at the same time?* If it will be quilted by a group, plan a quilting format that several people can easily follow without having to shift seating positions. The fan pattern shown here is an old-time favorite for church-group quilters because the lines form an arc, and one person can complete several lines of stitching without having to physically move down the side of the quilt.

Fan quilting fills the border of "Eliza's Star" by Jeana Kimball, 1999 (collection of Eliza Gutke).

◆ *Do you enjoy the hand-quilting process?* We all have our favorite and least-enjoyed parts of the quilt-making process. If your favorite is the rhythmic stitching of the layers together, quilt as densely as you like. When Marella Baker shared her mother's quilts with me, she said that as a girl she was embarrassed to invite her friends to her house because her mother, Florence Jane Stockdale, always had a quilt on the frame. The quilt frame took up the entire dining room and, in her mind, looked shabby.

As Marella grew older and wiser, she realized that the quilt on the frame served two important roles for her mother. First, it provided artistic expression while designing and drafting the patchwork and quilting patterns, and second, the hours her mother spent stitching at the frame were part of a healing process from some deep emotional pain. Florence Stockdale's quilts are beautifully and densely quilted, with approximately 15 stitches per inch. The quilt "Winding Ways" on page 38 was made by Florence for her second grandchild in 1930.

If your least favorite part of quiltmaking is the hand-quilting process, you may want to plan your quilt top to minimize the quilting detail. Some ways to do this include the following:

◆ Use fewer plain fabrics. Solid fabrics highlight quilting stitches, so substitute two-color fabrics that look like solids from a distance.

◆ Plan narrow borders that do not require large amounts of quilting to fill them.

◆ Choose quilting formats that avoid seams to make the stitching go faster, such as outline quilting or straight-set grid quilting (see pages 17–18).

Types of Quilting Designs

THERE ARE THREE basic types of quilting designs: plain block designs, border designs, and fill-in designs.

Plain block designs are used to fill in large, plain areas, such as a plain block set between two patchwork or appliqué blocks. There are many good reference books with quilting patterns and designs for these large areas. Check with your local quilt shop for a selection of quilt-pattern books.

Border designs are used to fill border strips with interesting quilting that highlights and complements the pattern used in the body of the quilt. There are some good reference books and plastic templates available to make this selection process easier. For a discussion of how to make templates for transferring your design to the quilt top, see page 57. A selection of cable quilting designs, which are popular for borders, is shown on pages 58–59.

Fill-in designs are used over the entire quilt top to tie together plain or empty places with quilting on the patchwork blocks and border. Also included in this general heading of fill-in designs is quilting done on patchwork blocks to enhance the patchwork design.

Read through the following types of quilting designs and the way they are used in quilts. Think about the ways you can make use of these various quilting designs in your own quilts.

Plain Block Designs

PLAIN BLOCK designs were traditionally derived from nature themes. Leaves were gathered and arranged in a pleasing format and then traced for quilting. In *Quilts in America,* Patsy and Myron Orlofsky tell of one quilter whose "mother and grandmother used to pick sprays of oak leaves, ivy, clover, and thistles, bringing them home to study in the evening, before making the decision of which should form the basis for a quilting design."[12] They also note that "acanthus leaves were a much-used motif by early American craftsmen. Many late eighteenth- and nineteenth-century houses have acanthus carvings around their fireplaces and on the inside of the front door."[13] It is very logical that a woman would look to elements in her environment for ideas of how to enhance the appearance of her quilts.

Other American motifs with symbolic traditions, such as the pineapple, lyre, and eagle, were also favorite quilting design inspirations. Very early whole-cloth quilts often started with a bouquet of flowers in a medallion-quilting format.

The rose is a traditional English quilting motif. It often resembles an American Dresden Plate patchwork-and-appliqué quilt pattern. Plain spaces on a Dresden Plate quilt, as shown below, were filled with such a rose pattern. A pattern for this rose appears on page 60.

Dresden Plate Design

11

One trick used by skilled quiltmakers to make their quilting motifs stand out is to stitch a second row—sometimes called double quilting—around the motif's outside edge. Stitch the second (or double) line about ⅛" to ¼" away from the first line for the best effect of setting the motif off from the fill-in quilting format.

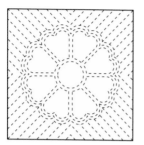

Double Quilting

Another English design from the "North Country" is the True Lover's Knot. While traditionally used on whole-cloth quilts or in plain areas, the photo below shows that it is effective on pieced designs as well. As you can guess from its name, the True Lover's Knot was frequently used on wedding quilts. Other traditional wedding-quilt motifs include baskets of flowers for happiness, grapes symbolizing plenty, and a chain continued unbroken around the corners to give a long life, with horseshoes to bring good luck.[14] There are patterns for a Pineapple and an 8" True Lover's Knot on pages 60 and 62.

True Lover's Knot in "Evening Star Sampler"

When deciding whether to use a motif with rounded or angular edges for plain areas in your quilt, try cutting a template from paper for each type and placing it on the quilt top to see the mood each creates. Rounded shapes, such as the rose mentioned earlier, will soften sharp points of pieced designs, while angular shapes, such as a star, heighten the effect of piecework. In general, most quilting motifs have rounded edges to make the quilting stitch flow smoothly. See pages 57–63 for further information about making templates and marking quilting designs.

Border Designs

WELL-PLANNED border quilting can finish your quilt into a cohesive, well-organized whole. Poorly planned border quilting, on the other hand, can make an entire quilt top seem unbalanced. Consider the following four types of formats when choosing a quilting design that will work well for a particular quilt.

DIAGONAL LINES

Diagonal-line formats can be used to fill border areas with straight lines of quilting. Below are two examples of diagonal fill-in designs for borders. Notice that on quilt A the diagonal lines change direction at the center of the border, while on quilt B they change direction at the corner.

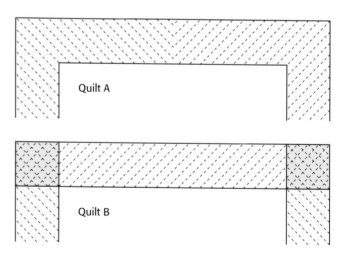

One advantage to using a diagonal fill-in format is that corners are easily managed. When using diagonal lines in the border (or as a background fill-in), it is important that the diagonal lines change direction rather than running in one direction only around (or across) the entire quilt. For example, if diagonal lines were all stitched from the top right corner to the lower left corner, it would cause the entire quilt to pull off-grain in the direction the quilting lines were stitched. This kind of distortion is common in needlepoint. Finished needlepoint can be blocked to square the shape, but a quilt cannot be rigidly blocked without the possibility of breaking threads in some of the quilting lines. Therefore, when planning to quilt diagonal lines, remember to change directions at regular intervals, usually once on each side.

Marking by hand, even with a ruler, yields inconsistencies. It's likely that the measurement between lines will not work out perfectly, no matter how carefully you plan. Some fudging is usually required to make lines come together at the required intervals. Although no one talks much about it, fudging is something that every quiltmaker needs to do at one time or another. Making small adjustments here and there to ensure that everything comes out correctly in the finished quilt is perfectly acceptable.

Changing Direction in the Middle of a Border

To mark diagonal fill-in lines that change direction in the middle of the border, follow these steps.

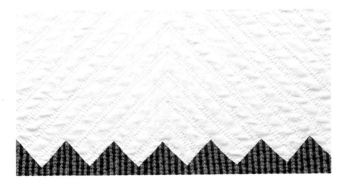

"Fairmeadow" features the "quilt A" border style shown in the diagram on page 12.

1. Start drawing lines in one corner and work toward the border center.

2. About 3" to 4" before reaching the center, stop and measure the actual distance from the last line marked to the center. If the measurement is not an even multiple of the spacing width you are using, start fudging as you mark each of the next few lines, so that they are wider or narrower than the regular intervals. By fudging this way over several lines, you can make the lines appear evenly spaced.

3. Repeat steps 1 and 2 at the opposite corner of the same border.

4. Continue marking the remaining borders in the same manner.

Overlapping Diagonal Lines at Corners

To mark diagonal fill-in lines that overlap at the corners, follow these steps.

"Hexagon Rose" features the "quilt B" border style shown in the diagram on page 12.

1. Begin at one border corner and mark a diagonal line from the outside corner of the border to the corner where the border is joined to the quilt center.

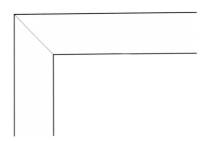

2. In one direction only, mark continuing diagonal lines along the border length, spacing them at the desired interval.

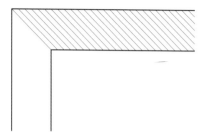

3. As you approach the next corner, place a piece of masking tape (or a lightly marked line) that visually extends the length of the current border to the raw edge of the quilt top. Continue marking diagonal lines to the corner, without crossing the masking-tape barrier.

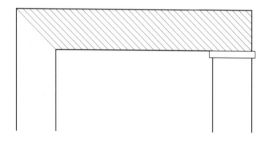

4. Reposition the masking tape as shown and repeat steps 1–3 to mark the adjacent border, overlapping (or crossing) the lines just marked at the corner. Take care to mark only to the edge of the masking tape in the corner area. This will result in cross-hatched corners and will automatically change the direction of the diagonal quilting lines for the second border.

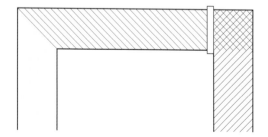

5. Repeat steps 1–4 around all four edges of the quilt border, ending at the corner where you began. At this corner, there will be a few crossed lines to finish marking.

Changing Direction at the Corner Miter

Another possibility for changing the direction of quilting lines is to use the corner as a guide. The quilt shown here had the advantage of a diagonal striped background, which served as an accurate guide for the quilting lines, each spaced ½" apart. This format could easily be marked with a ruler.

In "Country Life Album," striped fabric guided quilter Marian Baker to a perfectly finished miter. The full quilt is shown on page 44.

DISJOINTED DESIGNS

Another treatment to consider is the disjointed border design, in which a motif is repeated without touching the other motifs along the border length. Again, corners are easy to mark with this type of design because the space between motifs can be expanded or shortened, depending on the area to be filled. Below is a traditional Acanthus Leaf design used in a disjointed border, with the motif placed diagonally at the corner. A full-size pattern for the Acanthus motif is provided on page 61.

Evenly space large motifs in the borders.

CABLES

The third and most common type of border design is the cable. This border must be planned in advance to make corners turn smoothly. Cables can be somewhat difficult to mark when lap quilting, because lap designs are usually marked as you go. There are many variations of this linked-type border. Eight are shown below and in template form on pages 58 and 59.

Cable Border Designs

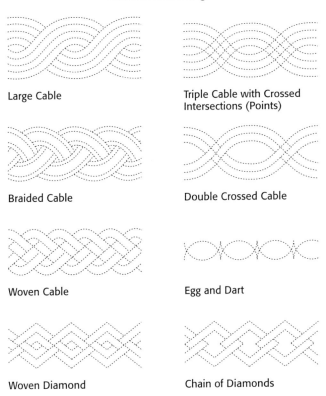

Large Cable

Triple Cable with Crossed Intersections (Points)

Braided Cable

Double Crossed Cable

Woven Cable

Egg and Dart

Woven Diamond

Chain of Diamonds

Advance planning is required to make motifs land at corners in the proper position. If the cable you are using is large or the repeats are 4" apart or more, you must measure the length of the border before beginning to mark and then adjust the size of the template so that the repeats will work out correctly. You can use the enlarging or reducing features on a photocopy machine in 5% or 10% increments to adjust the size of the template. For example, if you have a 6" repeat and the border measures 50" in length, adjust the template so that it repeats every 5" instead, and then ten repeats will fit the border perfectly.

Begin marking at one corner; continue across two-thirds of the border, and then stop and measure the distance to the next corner. Divide that number by the measurement of the repeat. Either expand or con-

dense the template design as you mark to fit the remaining space. This method allows you to begin adjusting early, so that the fudging isn't noticeable. The quilted design is secondary to the patchwork or appliqué of the quilt top, and you can easily disguise minor adjustments.

Cable Corner Designs

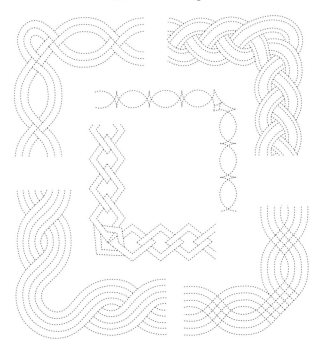

FEATHERS

Feather quilting designs are similar to cables. You can expand feathered designs to fill a very wide border, or you can straighten them out to suit a narrow one.

A feather pattern fills the "Whig Rose" border.

Follow these steps to plan a simple feathered vine.

1. Use freezer paper or smaller sheets of paper taped together to make a paper pattern that equals one-quarter or one-half of the quilt's finished border.

2. Fold the paper pattern into equal sections. The folds divide the pattern into sections that will be filled proportionately with the feather design.

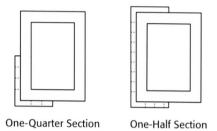

One-Quarter Section   One-Half Section

3. Draw a line through the center of the length of the master pattern. Next, draw a curved line that flows evenly through the divided sections.

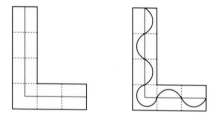

4. Use a light box to transfer the flowing center line onto the border of the quilt top before you layer the top with the batting and backing.

5. Use an individual feather template from page 61 to mark feathers along the flowing line you traced onto the quilt top. There is no need to premark the entire border. Feathers can be marked as you stitch, which makes this design a great one for lap or hoop quilting.

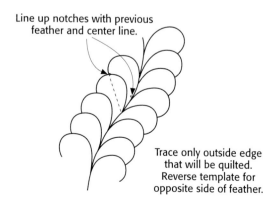

Line up notches with previous feather and center line.

Trace only outside edge that will be quilted. Reverse template for opposite side of feather.

The feathers can run in one direction continuously around the border or change directions at the corners as shown. When changing directions at the corners, the feather line must stop halfway along the length of the border, making a broken feather border like those often used in Amish quilts.

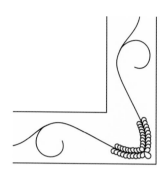

Trace the feather design directly onto the quilt top. You may mark the individual feathers along the premarked, flowing center line before the quilt is put on the frame, or you may mark it as you quilt, marking a few plumes at a time just ahead of your stitching. I prefer to mark as I stitch, using light marking lines, since there is no risk of the lines fading or flaking off before I quilt them. Begin marking in a corner and continue around the quilt. Many variations in feather quilting are possible when you use a disjointed vine that turns up, down, and back on itself as shown in the illustrations below and above. Experiment with a few variations to determine which one is best for your quilt.

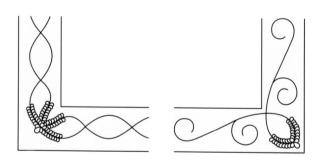

Fill-In Designs

Fill-in designs provide background transition between quilted elements or function as unobtrusive quilting in areas where the patchwork design is meant to dominate.

The 18 designs that follow are fill-in designs. You can mark many of them with a ruler, but some require the use of easily made templates. Notice how the same pieced block turns into something different with each fill-in variation.

QUILTING IN THE DITCH

Quilting in the ditch is an outline quilting method in which quilted lines follow the patchwork seams. Some quilters prefer to stitch so close to the seam lines that it is unnoticeable on the finished quilt top. Others prefer stitching slightly outside the seams, which allows the stitches to be visible and creates less stress on the seams. Either method of outline quilting is acceptable. Plan this type of quilting so that you are stitching along the seam line on the side where there are no seam allowances. (Seams are pressed to one side in most patchwork piecing.)

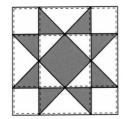

Quilting in the ditch is done along patchwork seam lines where there are no seam allowances.

OUTLINE QUILTING

Outline quilting is placed approximately ¼" from the pieced seam line. There are two reasons for using this method. First, it allows you to avoid stitching near or through any seam allowances. Second, the quilted line stands out and adds texture to the patchwork surface by echoing the lines of the patchwork. Outline quilting can also be used around appliqué shapes. However, the raised parts of a quilt receive more wear, so it may be a good idea to combine this type of outline quilting with quilting in the ditch.

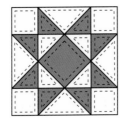

Outline quilting ¼" from seam line echoes and enhances the shapes.

In-the-Ditch and Outline Quilting in "Evening Star Sampler"

STRAIGHT-SET GRID

For on-point settings, another format that avoids seams is the straight-set grid. Vertical and horizontal lines are stitched over on-point patchwork, forming a simple grid like the ones found on graph paper (versus cross-hatching, which forms a diagonal, on-point grid). The stitching runs against the fabric grain (along the bias), parallel to the edges of the quilt. Candidates for this type of quilting include pieced designs that are set on point, such as Ocean Waves, Trip around the World, and Double Irish Chain.

The straight-set grid is a good format for on-point designs.

ON-GRAIN QUILTING

This type of quilting is stitched along the straight grain of the fabric. The stitches have a tendency to merge into the fabric, making them recede visually. I found this format useful when stitching the plain border areas behind the appliquéd letters in my "Come Berrying" quilt, shown on page 30. On-grain quilting doesn't draw up a quilt the same way that quilting across the grain does. When combined with other formats that do draw up a quilt, on-grain quilting can make the quilted surface look uneven. See page 31 to find out how I solved this problem when planning the quilting for "Come Berrying."

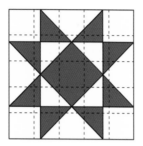

Straight-grid quilting follows the lengthwise and crosswise grain of the quilt top.

DIAGONAL LINES

A diagonal-line format is most often used to fill border areas. It is also used as fill-in quilting. It is one of my favorite formats for background quilting behind appliqué motifs, because the multiple diagonal lines give the impression of a more time-consuming format, such as cross-hatching.

Plan diagonal-line quilting so the lines change direction in order to avoid distorting the quilt top when stitching.

Diagonal-Line Quilting in "Evening Star Sampler"

ECHO QUILTING

Echo quilting is traditionally used on Hawaiian quilts and occasionally on other appliqué quilts. In fact, it is often referred to as Hawaiian quilting. Quilted lines begin at the edge of the appliqué, and successive rows of stitching beyond the first row echo the shape. The rule of thumb for spacing this kind of quilting is a finger's width apart. However, any distance less than that is also acceptable. Spacing rows any farther apart than a finger's width may cause the echo effect to disappear.

Echo quilting echoes the appliqué shape in each successive row.

Echo Quilting in "Baltimore Basket" by Jeana Kimball, 1988

CROSS-HATCHING

Cross-hatching describes diagonal quilting lines that create squares on the quilt. First, mark a large X on the quilt top, drawing the lines from corner to corner across the center surface of a square quilt, or across a square portion of a rectangular quilt. Then, mark additional lines parallel to the X lines. The most commonly used distance between lines for this type of quilting is ½" to 1".

Cross-hatching covers the quilt with
closely spaced rows of diagonal quilting.

Cross-Hatching in "Evening Star Sampler"

CROSS-HATCHING VARIATIONS

Sometimes double lines—and occasionally triple
lines—are used in cross-hatching to emphasize the
quilting. Another variation is to create the look of a
plaid by varying the number of lines and the distance
between them. This variation can either be set in
straight lines parallel to the edges of the quilt top or on
the diagonal.

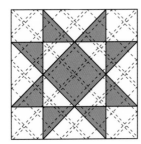

Closely spaced double rows for cross-hatching
add more emphasis to the quilted surface.
When double rows are used alternately
rather than over the entire surface,
a "plaid" quilting design emerges.

Plaid Cross-Hatching Variation in "Evening Star Sampler"

UNCROSSED LINES

This method of fill-in quilting is done in a grid of
straight lines, but none of them ever cross each other.
When quilt blocks are placed next to each other and
quilted in this format, it creates interesting surface texture. Another option is to change the direction of the
uncrossed lines, which also creates interesting visual
texture.

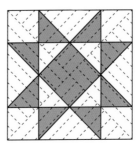

Changing the direction of uncrossed lines
adds visual movement to the quilt surface.

Uncrossed Lines in "Evening Star Sampler"

HANGING DIAMONDS

This diagonal-line quilting format creates a hanging-diamond pattern on the quilt surface. It is an easy pattern to mark on a quilt top. First, draw parallel lines along the length of the quilt top and then draw a second set of lines on the diagonal across the surface. Space the lines in both directions the same width apart. In this example, double lines were marked approximately ⅛" apart to emphasize the diamond shapes.

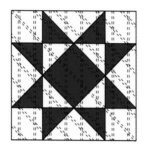

A hanging diamond quilting pattern
is easy to mark on the quilt top.

Hanging Diamonds in "Evening Star Sampler"

DIAMONDS

In this format, vertical diamond shapes are created on the surface of the quilt. To establish the line spacing and the correct angle for the diamond format, draft a diamond-shaped template in the size you desire. Then place the template in the center of the quilt top and

trace. Using a yardstick, extend the lines to the outer edges of the quilt top. Continue drawing parallel lines across the surface of the quilt, making the space between the lines the same as the length of one leg of the diamond.

Trace diamond-shaped template in center
of quilt, then extend lines to outer edges.

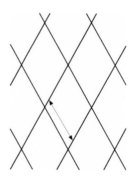

Measure diamond leg
indicated by arrow
to establish line spacing.

Vertical Diamonds in "Evening Star Sampler"

WAVE OR HERRINGBONE

This undulating design is based on an equilateral triangle (all three sides equal). Make a triangle template in the size you desire. Use this template to mark the vertical rows of zigzag quilting lines.

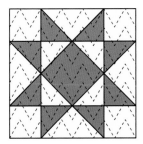

Wave or herringbone design requires only one triangular template.

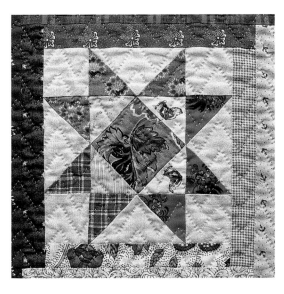

Waves in "Evening Star Sampler"

BASKET WEAVE OR SPLINT

In *Old Patchwork Quilts and the Women Who Made Them,* Ruth Finley says that the basket-weave design required so much accuracy in marking that it was very early discarded as too difficult to be worthwhile.[15] It is true that it is difficult to mark, but taking the time to carefully plan and mark your design will enable you to create a very charming finished quilting design. Choose one of the three variations that follow, leaving spaces and marking lines as indicated. This design looks especially nice on a basket or floral appliqué quilt.

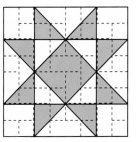

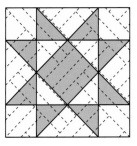

Basket Weave in "Amish Whole Cloth Medallion"

FAN

This design is frequently found on old scrap quilts, because this type of quilt was often the subject of a quilting bee. The fan format allowed many people to work at a quilting frame at the same time without having to shift positions frequently.

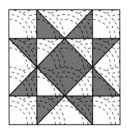

The fan is also easy to mark, using either a string and a pencil or a series of fan-shaped templates in increasingly larger sizes. To mark with a pencil and string, first tie knots along a length of string, evenly spacing the knots ½" apart. Then wrap the end of the string around a pencil with enough of the string let out to reach the first knot. Draw the arc. Then, unwrap the string to the next knot. Start in a corner of the quilt and mark along one side. Continue until you have marked the desired number of fan repeats.

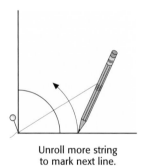

Unroll more string
to mark next line.

Fans in "Evening Star Sampler"

This marking and quilting format works nicely when quilting at an old-fashioned four-rail quilting frame. The sides of the quilt that are rolled on the rails are marked with the fan pattern, building one row upon the previous row. Traditionally, frame quilters would work and mark from opposite sides of the quilt frame toward the center. No attempt is made to make the rows of fans join or connect in any way at the quilt center; the quilted fans simply butt up to one another. Old-time quiltmakers refer to this center area, where the fans stitched from opposite sides meet, as the spine of the quilt. And, indeed, it is usually the center of the quilt.

CLAMSHELL

This traditional fill-in design gives a pleasing curved effect to a quilted surface. A half-circle template with a notch in the middle of the arc makes marking this design an easy task. This format was also used on my quilt "Rabbit Patch" on page 33. See the discussion on page 32 to learn why and how this was the format of choice.

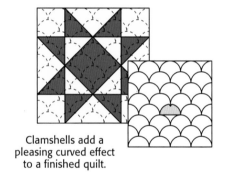

Clamshells add a
pleasing curved effect
to a finished quilt.

Double Clamshells in "Evening Star Sampler"

TEACUP OR WINEGLASS

In this design, a series of overlapping circles creates the optical illusion of a four-petal flower at first glance. At second glance, circles appear. Early methods of marking this format employed a teacup or wineglass, hence the name. As Ruth Finley reminds us in *Old Patchwork Quilts,* older teacups had no handles to get in the way of marking.[16] The template used to mark this design was a circle with four notches at equal intervals around it to indicate when the overlap is in the correct position.

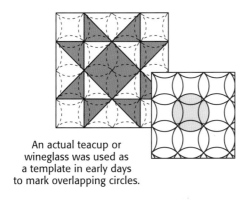

An actual teacup or wineglass was used as a template in early days to mark overlapping circles.

Teacups in "Evening Star Sampler"

STIPPLING

For those who truly enjoy the quilting process, stipple quilting is perfect. Stipple quilting means covering the entire surface with quilting stitches so densely spaced that hardly a stitch can fit between them. Stipple quilting is most often found on appliqué and whole-cloth quilts. One method of stipple quilting is to echo quilt with only ¹⁄₁₆" between each row of stitches. Another method is to randomly stitch over the surface until the entire area is filled. In the quilt shown above right,

Eleanor Tracy's strategy was to echo alternately from the outside edges of the border and appliqué motifs.

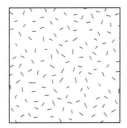

Stipple stitches are placed randomly and very close together.

Stippling in "Album Quilt"

CONTINUOUS-LINE DESIGNS

Continuous-line designs are very popular among both hand and machine quilters and are adaptable to long-arm quilting machines. Machine and hand quilters alike find these designs easy to stitch because they require few stops and starts. For more information on this design, see "Resources" on page 80.

Trapunto

T F YOU WISH to add extra dimension and texture to a quilt, you may use a technique called trapunto, or stuff work. In this method (also known as "Italian" quilting), two layers of fabric are sewn together along selected design lines to outline the area that will be stuffed. Then the area is stuffed from the back of the quilt with a lightweight padding or cording.

Trapunto was frequently used on whole-cloth "best quilts" in earlier centuries. Traditionally, a fine, tightly woven grade of cotton fabric was used for the quilt top, and a coarser, more loosely woven cotton—sometimes handwoven by the quiltmaker—was used for the backing. After the outline of the stuffed design was quilted, the threads of the quilt backing were separated with a stiletto (a sewing tool about the length of a toothpick with a pointed end), and tiny bits of stuffing were inserted into the desired areas.

After the stuffing was completed, the backing fibers were moved back into place with the stiletto point, so that little or no evidence remained to indicate how the stuffing was inserted. Some quiltmakers would cut a slit through the backing, insert the stuffing, and then use a whipstitch to rejoin the cut edges of the backing. This last method took less time but was considered less desirable because the back of the quilt was not as attractive.

To stuff narrow, linear, or curved areas, such as flower stems and basket handles, or self-contained designs with curved channels, such as a True Lover's Knot motif (page 62), a slightly different method was used. First, the design lines were quilted through both layers of fabric. Then a blunt needle, such as a tapestry needle, was threaded with yarn and inserted into the stitched channel through the quilt backing. After guiding the needle and yarn through the channel, the needle was gently pushed out through the backing and the yarn was cut at both ends. The yarn ends were manipulated into the channel, using either the stiletto

or the point of the needle. When carefully done, no sign existed of where the yarn entered or exited the channel.

Guide blunt needle
through quilted seam channel.

Both of these trapunto techniques are still in use today. Another variation called shadow work is also done. A sheer or transparent fabric is used for the quilt top, and the design areas are stuffed with brightly colored yarns. The color that shadows through the quilt top is a pastel version of the yarns used.

Jeanne Huber's beautiful quilt "Tall Trees," shown on page 39, is an excellent example of a modern quilt featuring trapunto. Some of the trapunto techniques she used are different than those described above, but they are more applicable for today's quiltmaking because the types of fabrics used by earlier quiltmakers are no longer available. Jeanne does the trapunto on the completed quilt top before layering the top with batting and backing. When you use her method, there is no need to make holes or cut slits in the quilt backing in order to add the stuffing.

1. For each design area selected for trapunto quilting, cut a piece of very fine, lightweight fabric, such as lawn or batiste, making sure that it is slightly larger all around than the actual design motif.

2. Using a pencil, trace the selected design onto the lightweight fabric and baste it in place on the back of the quilt top, with the pencil tracing facing you. It is important to note that if the design is asymmetrical, you will need to make a reverse tracing; otherwise, the finished design on the

quilt top will be a reverse image of the design you have chosen.

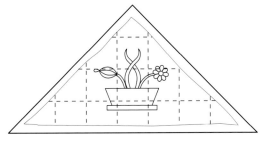

Baste traced design in place.

3. Thread a needle with thread in a light but contrasting color and tie a knot at one end. Insert the needle through the right side of the quilt top at the end of one of the pencil lines, so that the knot will be on the surface of the quilt top. Bring the thread to the wrong side of the quilt top and outline the trapunto motif with fairly small basting stitches. Do not make these stitches as small as your hand-quilting stitches. The basting stitches will be replaced with actual quilting stitches when the rest of the top is quilted.

4. To stuff the basted areas, carefully make small slits in the lightweight fabric only. Then stuff small bits of polyester batting through the slits or draw cording through basted channels. Jeanne Huber recommends using the points of a small pair of embroidery scissors to gently push the batting into place. Note that overstuffing areas with batting or using a yarn that is too large in diameter causes design distortion and a lumpy appearance. The goal is a softly stuffed look.

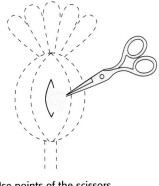

Use points of the scissors to stuff motif.

5. Loosely whipstitch the slits back together to keep the batting in place. In the case of cording, it is not necessary to manipulate the yarn ends into the channels, since the back of the work will be completely covered by the quilt batting and backing.

6. Layer the quilt top with batting and backing and baste. Quilt as desired. In the areas where the stuffing has been added, quilt just inside the basted lines. After these quilting stitches are completed, carefully remove the basting stitches around each motif.

Loop Yarn around Curves

When inserting cording into designs with tight curves or when turning sharp corners, bring the needle with yarn out of the channel on the wrong side of the quilt top. Reinsert the needle into the same hole, leaving a small loop of yarn on the back side of the quilt top. This technique makes it easier to insert the cording around curves and helps prevent puckers and pulls on the surface.

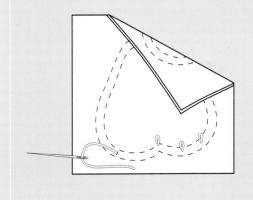

Quilting an Appliqué Quilt

IN MY QUILTMAKING career I have focused on appliqué design. It has been my goal to have the quilts I make share the timeless quality that many antique quilts possess. To achieve this goal, I have studied all I can about the techniques and materials that women of the nineteenth century would have used for their quilts. In this section I outline what I learned and what I try to incorporate into the quilts I make.

My study of the quilting on antique quilts is an ongoing journey of discovery. The most important thing I have learned is to make no assumptions as to how a particular aspect was usually handled. I have "unlearned" many things I thought I knew, simply by taking the time to notice what quiltmakers had done in the nineteenth century.

Materials

GENERALLY, APPLIQUÉ quilts were made as "best" quilts. A woman may have made only one such quilt in her lifetime. Her purpose in making this quilt was not to make a warm bedcover for her family, but to visually warm the heart and exhibit her needlework skill.

She would have purchased all new material for this important quilt. She would not have "made do" with materials she had on hand. She bought the best fine, tightly woven background fabric she could afford, but the backing material was often handwoven or of a looser weave than the front. This served well if she were planning to add trapunto or stuff work to her design.

The batting was always a very thin layer of cotton, which allowed the quilter to showcase her tiny, even quilting stitches. She most likely carded the batting to remove seeds and to untangle and carefully position the fibers into a fine layer, knowing full well that it would be quilted heavily. As discussed in "Choosing the Batting" on pages 65–67, the batting I have found that comes closest to this is Mountain Mist Blue Ribbon batting, split to create a very thin layer. A thicker layer of batting wouldn't show the level of quilting detail that is so prevalent on antique appliqué quilts.

Background Formats

THE BACKGROUND quilting on antique appliqué quilts was often intended to recede, allowing the appliqué to come forward. Surprisingly, cross-hatching was not the usual background choice. When I have seen it used, I found that large, white areas of cross-hatch quilting tend to attract attention rather than recede into the background. There is something about the regular pattern of diagonal crossed lines that attracts the eye. When cross-hatching is used in the background, my eye is drawn as quickly to the quilting as it is to the appliqué design.

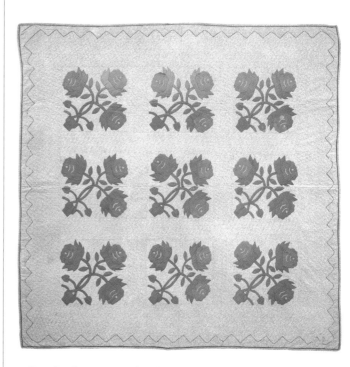

Cross-hatching was used in background areas of "Potted Roses" by unknown maker, third quarter of nineteenth century, Pennsylvania, 86½" x 86½". (Collection of Judy Roche.)

Cross-Hatching in "Potted Roses"

A more common background solution seen on antique quilts is an irregular format, such as leaves and tendrils or feather plumes and circles. These soft shapes fill large open areas and are sometimes supplemented by diagonal-line quilting or cross-hatching.

Irregular background quilting in "Whig Rose with Center Basket Design" by unknown maker, third quarter of nineteenth century, Pennsylvania. (Collection of Judy Roche.)

Outline Quilting

AN ASSUMPTION I made about appliqué quilts was that in order to enhance the appliqué design, quilting should surround the shapes to make them pop out for a dimensional look. After examining many antique appliqué quilts and giving the issue some logical thought, I learned that this theory is not necessarily correct. Many old quilts do have outline quilting around the appliqué motifs, but many others do not.

In some quilts the background quilting goes right up to the edge of the appliqué shapes without going around them. Initially, I did this on a quilt for which I had a completion deadline. The quilt looked as heavily quilted as any other quilt on which I'd used outline quilting and it took less time. I liked the format so well that I no longer outline quilt any of my appliqué motifs.

Background quilting extends to the edges of appliqué motifs in "One Fine Day."

In other antique quilts, the background quilting continues over the appliqué shapes, as if they were part of the background fabric.

"Oak Leaf and Reel" by unknown maker, mid-nineteenth century, Bucks County, Pennsylvania. (Collection of Judy Roche.)

Even more strangely, sometimes the quiltmaker outline quilted on top of the appliqué shapes. This required her to stitch not only through the backing, batting, and background fabric, but also through the appliqué fabric and the turned-under seam allowance as well!

While analyzing why this was done, I realized that women in the nineteenth century, who used quilts only on their beds, knew much more about how quilts wear out than I ever could. One strand of thread, stitched just once around an appliqué shape, is the only support that the appliqué piece has to hold it in place on the quilt. Quilting on top of appliqué shapes reinforces the single strand of thread holding them in

place, and the quilting stitches force the appliqués down against the background, so that they are flatter and better supported against wear.

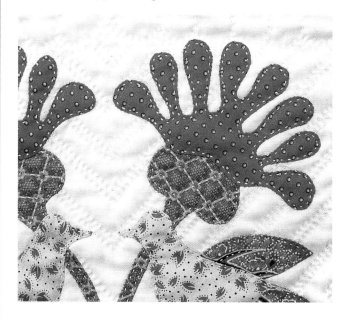

Appliqué pieces are quilted along their edges in "Forget-Me-Knots" by Jeana Kimball, 2003.

If you closely examine the wear pattern on your quilts, you will see that the areas that first begin to show wear are the uppermost pieces. Appliqué is always the top layer, making it the area most prone to wear.

Wear shows on "Coxcomb and Currants" by unknown maker, mid-nineteenth century. (Collection of the author.)

Border Quilting

ANOTHER INTERESTING aspect of the quilting done on antique appliqué quilts is the format chosen for the border. Even though the same fabrics were used in the border and in the body of the quilt, usually without a break between them, the border features a different quilting format than the quilt center. Perhaps this was to make the border stand out and visually frame the center of the quilt. The format chosen for the border was often diagonal lines (many times double-line quilting) and a feather design. Using the shape of the appliquéd vine as the spine of the feather design, the individual plumes were marked and stitched over the appliqué flowers and leaves in the border. The feather quilting overlapped the flowers and leaves of the vine as if they were not there.

It could well be that the diagonal-line quilting in the border was chosen because it would draw up the center of the quilt evenly, making all of the edges straight and flat.

Border quilting in "Whig Rose." For a full view of the quilt, see page 45.

Understanding the Design Process

I N THIS SECTION I describe the thought processes I went through as I planned the quilting for my quilts "Come Berrying" and "Rabbit Patch." You will see how I analyzed the elements in each quilt and determined the scale, proportion, and size of the quilting formats. Use this same type of thought process to define your quilting strategy and select quilting formats for your own quilts.

Come Berrying

I LIKE to keep quilting in proportion to the size of the quilt. For a quilt top that is 45" x 45" or smaller, I suggest small intervals between quilting lines: ½" would be my choice. My quilt top for "Come Berrying" measured 54" x 54", which meant that the quilting lines could be farther apart. To decide on the quilting intervals for this

"Come Berrying" by Jeana Kimball, 1994, Ivins, Utah, 53" x 53". (Collection of the author.)

quilt, I started by analyzing the elements of the quilt and looked for logical places to stitch quilting lines.

One of the first strategies in planning quilting is to avoid stitching on seam allowances as much as possible. Stitching on seams slows down the quilting process and makes it difficult to maintain small, even stitches. The 1" squares in the checkerboard borders of "Come Berrying" contain many seam allowances. To avoid quilting over them, the logical choice was to quilt diagonal lines across the checkerboard. The quilting lines would intersect seams at the corner of each square, but the greater part of the square (diagonally across its surface) would be seam-free and easy to quilt. As I contemplated this area of the quilt, I also realized that the distance between the diagonal lines of quilting would measure ¾". Thus I chose ¾" as the quilting interval to use throughout the quilt.

Diagonal background quilting mimics cross-hatching.

Diagonal quilting in the checkerboard border minimizes seam interference.

Quilting appliqué backgrounds can be problematic. The focus of the quilt is the appliqué. The background needs to be quilted, but the quilting should enhance the appliqué rather than detract from it. Cross-hatching is a common solution, but it is time-consuming. In "Come Berrying," I used a diagonal-line format that gave the impression of cross-hatching without requiring the time that cross-hatching takes. Having already determined that I would use a ¾"

interval between lines of quilting, I marked and quilted diagonal lines across each block, around the appliqué motifs.

I decided to quilt on top of my appliqués, to add dimension to the motifs and secure them more tightly to the quilt. For more information about quilting on top of appliqué shapes, see "Quilting an Appliqué Quilt" on page 26.

Quilting over appliqués adds textural interest and firmly anchors the motifs.

I left the red sashing between blocks and the green sashing between the checkerboard borders unquilted, except for quilting in the ditch along the seams. These areas weren't so large that batting migration was a concern, and nothing in them needed to be highlighted or emphasized with quilting.

The background area behind the appliqué lettering presented my next challenge. I felt that the background needed to recede, and that cross-hatching lines might be distracting or make the area appear busy. I chose on-grain straight lines quilted at ¾" intervals for this area, because quilting stitches that lie along the grain line of the fabric tend to merge or recede into the fabric. Note the way that the straight-line quilting fits into the corner.

In the white border, quilting stitches maintain a low profile by following the fabric grain.

It is important to recognize that the straight-line quilting format is successful because the checkerboard borders flank both sides of the lettering border. The diagonal-line quilting in the checkerboard borders drew up the lettering border in proportion to the quilting everywhere else on the quilt. If the appliqué lettering border had been the final border on this quilt, the outside edges of the quilt would have been wavy. As described on page 17, straight-line quilting parallel to the grain of the fabric does not draw up a quilt in the way that cross-grain quilting does.

The quilting on "Come Berrying" is visually pleasing because the amount of quilting is proportional to the overall size of the quilt, the intervals between the lines of quilting are uniform throughout, and the quilting formats enhance the appliqué shapes.

Rabbit Patch

My quilt "RABBIT PATCH" finished at 44" x 44". I considered it a small quilt and planned to place my quilting lines at ½" intervals, which is closer together than I would place them on a larger quilt such as "Come Berrying." "Rabbit Patch" is similar to "Come Berrying" in its combination of patchwork and appliqué, but the roles of these elements are reversed in "Rabbit Patch."

To plan my quilting strategy, I began with the patchwork basket. The 1" half-square triangles in the upper part of the Basket block were my first area of concentration. Here, seams were numerous and close together. I wanted to plan a quilting format that avoided the seams as much as possible. I rejected the traditional quilting-in-the-ditch format, because it did little to enhance the basket-filled-with-eggs theme of the quilt. I continued to study the patchwork, and in just a few minutes I realized that a traditional clamshell format would fit nicely over the "egg" triangles, complementing the quilt theme and, best of all, allowing me to avoid quilting over seams. Using a circle template (commonly used in appliqué to trace perfect circles), I found a circle size that would form a clamshell over the triangle. I made a plastic clamshell template, as shown on page 22, and began marking and quilting.

Quilted clamshells curve over multicolored triangles, avoiding seams.

"Rabbit Patch" by Jeana Kimball, 1993, Ivins, Utah, 44" x 44". (Collection of the author.)

Having already decided that diagonal-line quilting would be placed at ½" intervals, I marked and quilted cross-hatching lines in the basket portion of the pieced blocks.

Because I did not want to highlight the green sashing between Basket blocks or the narrow green border surrounding the pieced center, I left them unquilted, except for in-the-ditch quilting along the seams.

I repeated the clamshell theme across the quilt, using it as fill-in on the large half-square triangles used to square up the patchwork center. To enlarge the original clamshell, I quilted a second line ¼" outside the

Diagonal cross-hatching fills the on-point shape of the brown basket.

first marking. This double-line quilting reduced the number of clamshells needed to fill the large, plain triangles, and it made the quilting look more intricate.

For the appliqué border, I began with simple outline quilting around each rabbit. The appliqué motifs filled the border so tightly that no background quilting was needed to secure the border further. The only large areas left unquilted were the appliquéd bodies of the rabbits. In keeping with my theory that repeating quilting formats across the surface of a quilt gives it continuity, I chose to repeat the cross-hatching from the brown baskets on the rabbit bodies. Since there were no straight edges with which to align the cross-hatching, I used the template technique described on page 20 to mark a diamond quilting format. Using a ⅜" square template, I marked and stitched cross-hatching squares on the rabbits' bodies.

On the outermost pink and green borders, I repeated the double clamshell format. I quilted from the outside edge toward the inside, overlapping into the pink border and treating the two borders as one. The corners were managed by simply butting the clamshells against the mitered corner.

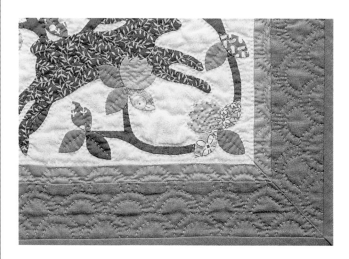

A continuous clamshell design covers the pink and green borders.

By repeating quilting formats from area to area, you accomplish two things: uniform density of quilting and continuity of design. If you keep both the scale of your quilting designs and the intervals between quilting lines proportional to the scale of the quilt design itself, you can guarantee that your quilting format will be a success.

Cross-hatching fills the rabbit appliqués. Straight lines quilted through the leaves and on clover blossoms add detail and keep the appliqués securely attached in the quilt border.

COXCOMB QUILT *by Donna Hanson Eines, 1997, Seattle, Washington, 80½" x 80½". To set off her lovely four-block appliqué quilt, Donna chose straight-line quilting set off with trapunto detail between the blocks. Quilting on top of the appliqué motifs adds dimension and detail to the quilt design. Notice the diagonal-line quilting in the borders that changes direction behind the vases. (Collection of the maker.)*

ALBUM QUILT, *by Eleanor Tracy, 1989, West Valley City, Utah, 74" x 92". Simple cross-hatching sets off the beautiful appliqué blocks in Eleanor's quilt. To highlight her elegant appliqué border design, Eleanor stipple quilted the border. (Collection of the maker.)*

EVENING STAR
SAMPLER *by Jeana
Kimball, 1992, Ivins, Utah,
34" x 42". Each block of this
wall quilt is quilted in a
different quilting format.
Detail photos of each of these
blocks are used to illustrate
"Types of Quilting Designs"
on pages 11–23. The quilt
has an interesting overall
texture created by the use of
the varied quilting formats.
(Collection of the author.)*

WINDING WAYS *by Florence Jane Stockdale, 1930, Colorado Springs, Colorado, 44" x 65 ½". Excellent pattern drafting and precise workmanship make this deceivingly simple-looking quilt a work of art. Notice the precisely curved lines of diamond quilting in the borders. Mrs. Stockdale made this quilt for her second grandchild. (Collection of Marella Baker, Salt Lake City, Utah.)*

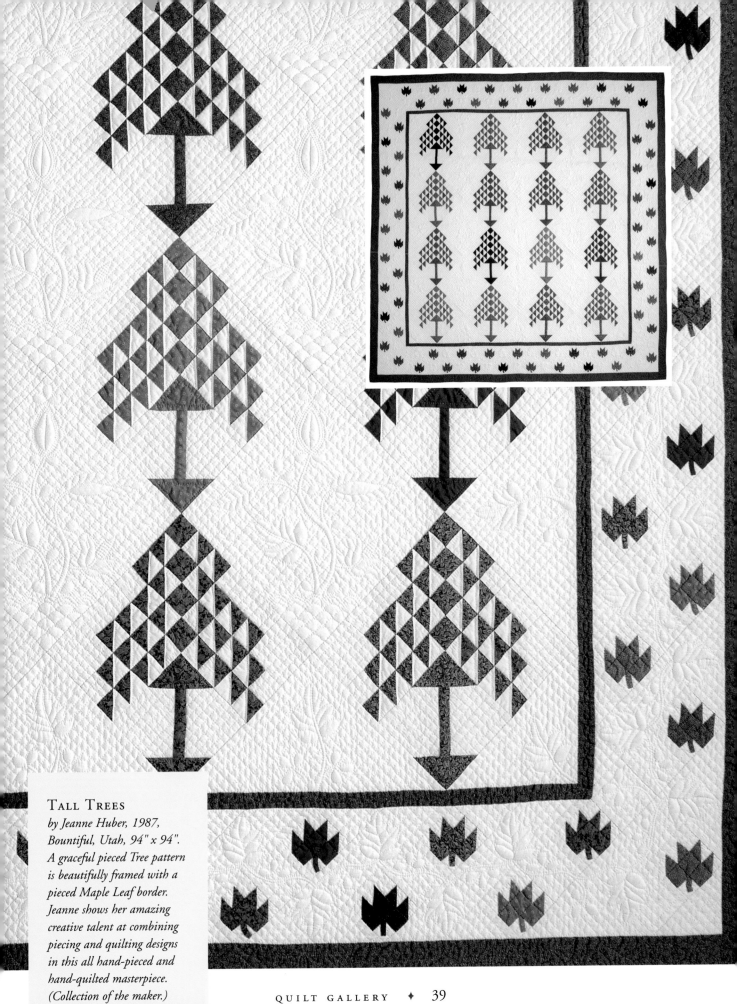

TALL TREES

by Jeanne Huber, 1987,
Bountiful, Utah, 94" x 94".
A graceful pieced Tree pattern
is beautifully framed with a
pieced Maple Leaf border.
Jeanne shows her amazing
creative talent at combining
piecing and quilting designs
in this all hand-pieced and
hand-quilted masterpiece.
(Collection of the maker.)

ELIZA'S STAR *by Jeana Kimball and Loraine Hoyt Jones, 1997, Ivins, Utah, 40" x 40". Fan quilting enhances a simple pieced star, stitched in vintage 1930s fabrics. The quilt top was designed and made by Eliza's grandmother and quilted by her great-grandmother. (Collection of Eliza Gutke.)*

PIECED MEDALLION
by unknown Quaker quilt-maker, 1863, Philadelphia, Pennsylvania, 84½" x 77¼". An impressive variety of silk fabrics are showcased in this one-of-a-kind pieced medallion. The remarkable pieced design is enhanced with equally creative use of botanical motifs in the quilting. (Collection of Judy Roche.)

OAK LEAF AND REEL

by unknown quiltmaker, mid-nineteenth century, Bucks County, Pennsylvania, 87" x 92". These classic combinations of red and green fabrics in a traditional Oak Leaf and Reel appliqué format are beautifully enhanced with remarkable quilting. The body of the quilt is quilted with an even ½" cross-hatching format that is stitched over the appliqué and pieced motifs as if they were not there. As the quilting continues into the border, the quiltmaker changed her format to 1" cross hatching with double lines. (Collection of Judy Roche.)

DIANTHA A. MYERS 1852.

DIANTHA A. MYERS 1852.

WEDDING QUILT
by Diantha A. Myers, 1852,
Central New York, 76" x 89".
With confidence and skill,
Diantha designed and quilted
this masterpiece that showcases
her competence in both
appliqué and quilting. Notice
how she left large open areas
in which to display her
quilting. (Collection of
Judy Roche.)

COUNTRY LIFE ALBUM *by Marian Baker, 2000, Salt Lake City, Utah, 82" x 96". A delightful collection of appliqué blocks are bordered with Marian's original border. The background fabric is a diagonal stripe that was cleverly utilized as a guide for placement of the quilting lines. The border is quilted the same way with the stripe changing directions on all sides of the quilt. (Collection of Marian Baker.)*

WHIG ROSE *by
unknown maker, 1852,
77" x 84". This lovely quilt
is a masterpiece of beautiful
quilting. A highly skilled
quiltmaker hid her first
name—Mary—and the
date between graceful feather
plumes and delicate grapevine
motifs, hand stitching the
entire surface of this quilt
with 15 to16 stitches per
inch. (Collection of Linda
Gabrielse.)*

AMISH WHOLE CLOTH MEDALLION

by unknown maker, Indiana, c. 1920, 68" x 85". Many traditional Amish quilting patterns are combined into a remarkable whole in this whole cloth medallion quilt. The satin weave of the subtle-colored cotton fabric highlights the beautiful stitching. (Collection of Linda Gabrielse.)

GRACE *by Charlotte Warr Anderson, 2000, Salt Lake City, Utah, 48" x 57". This commissioned work is a loving tribute to Grace Elizabeth Matthews Bagley at the request of her son, Jim Bagley. It was the influence of Grace that embarked Jim on his life-time career of designing and making quilting frames that meet the needs of hand quilters everywhere. Jim's company is the well-known Grace Frame Company. Featuring details of Grace's life, this quilt was beautifully hand appliquéd and hand quilted. (Collection of Jim Bagley.)*

ONE FINE DAY *by Jeana Kimball, 1996, Ivins, Utah, 33" x 41". Two sizes of cross-hatching set off the appliqué blocks in the center of this sweet quilt. Detail is added to the border with an ivy motif quilted in green thread. Straight-line quilting in white thread creates a background for the quilted green ivy, filling and flattening the remaining border area. (Collection of the author.)*

FAIRMEADOW *by Jeana Kimball, 1992, Ivins, Utah, 40" x 40". Diagonal line quilting sets off the appliqué designs in the quilt center. The red sashing between the blocks is quilted with a zigzag that echoes the appliqué dogtooth border that frames the quilt. (Collection of the author.)*

Quilting Tools

ALTHOUGH RELATIVELY FEW tools are required for hand quilting, it is important that the tools you use are both comfortable in your hands and effective for your preferred method of stitching. Because each quilter uses her hands differently, what works well for one person may not be satisfactory for another. Experiment with some or all the following tools to determine which ones give you the best results. The most important thing to remember is that, regardless of the tools you use or how you use them, a well-quilted quilt is your ultimate goal.

Needles

THE GENERAL rule of needle sizing is that the higher the number, the shorter the needle, the thinner the shank, and the smaller the eye. Some quilters believe that a size 12 Between is the best needle to use for hand quilting. However, no one needle size is exactly right for everyone. It is worthwhile to purchase a package of several different needle types and sizes and take the time to try each one. The following information will get you started.

BETWEENS

Betweens,
Actual Size

Originally designed for hand quilting at a frame, Betweens are shorter, thicker, and stronger than other hand-sewing needles. The thick shank makes it possible to take several stitches at a time through the three layers of a quilt sandwich without it bending. The thickness of the shank accommodates a larger eye than other needle types. New modifications are being added to some brands of needles, such as an embroidery eye for ease of threading and a double point (sharp on both ends, with an eye in the center) for stab-stitch quilting techniques.

SHARPS

Sharps,
Actual Size

Sharps are all-purpose, medium-length sewing needles. Traditionally, they are recommended for hemming, mending, sewing on buttons, and other basic sewing tasks. They have a longer, thinner shank and narrower eye than Betweens, but are still strong enough to use when quilting at a frame or in a hoop. Many quilt-makers consider them to be ideal for hand quilting.

STRAW NEEDLES

Straw Needles,
Actual Size

I have come to prefer Straw (or milliner's) needles over any other type of needle for hand quilting. Originally used in the hatmaking trade, these needles have a long shank and larger eye, which makes them perfect for stitching through things like ribbons, straw, and buckram. These needles are also great for hand quilting with cotton or specialty threads, such as pearl cotton, embroidery floss, and metallic threads.

I like the extra length of the size 8 Straw needle because it gives me more control over moving the needle through the layers of a quilt sandwich. I also avoid calluses on my fingers when I use this needle with my lap-quilting method.

In *Old Patchwork Quilts and the Women Who Made Them*, Ruth Finley says that early quilters used a "fairly long needle" for quilting. She also says that a curved needle was even better for quilting, and that "women always 'broke in' quilting needles by using them first on coarser every-day patchwork. Needles that became nicely bent were jealously saved for the curves and flourishes of the intricate needlework that was lavished on best quilts." [17] Other research supports Mrs. Finley's needle theory. For example, in *Traditional British Quilts,* Dorothy Osler says that when talking with one Welsh quilter, "she opened a piece of unfinished quilting, stored away since the 1930s, to reveal a long Sharps needle still threaded to the last line of stitches!" [18]

I suggest that you try different types and brands of needles to find the one you like best, because not all needles are alike from manufacturer to manufacturer, even though the size may be the same. Make it a practice to continue trying new needles every now and then. You may discover that your needle preferences change as your hand-quilting skills develop.

Thread

HAND-QUILTING thread is heavier than regular sewing thread because it must be strong enough to keep the layers of a quilt sandwich together and withstand wear if the quilt is put into daily use on a bed. Check the label to be sure you are buying "quilting" thread. Choose from 100%-cotton quilting thread or cotton-wrapped polyester quilting thread.

I prefer to use only 100% cotton thread for quilting because all of the components in my quilts—quilt top, batting, and backing—are also 100% cotton. However, many quilters prefer cotton-wrapped polyester thread because they believe it is stronger. Try both types in different brands and choose your favorite.

Needle Threaders

IF YOU have difficulty threading the small eye of the needle you like to use, a needle threader may be necessary. However, try the following suggestions first. They may eliminate the need for a needle threader.

♦ Always thread a freshly cut thread end. The thread fiber will be more tightly twisted at the newly cut end than at the end that has been exposed on the spool for a time. Make this fresh cut on the diagonal instead of straight across the thread. A diagonal cut is easier to thread through the eye of a needle.

♦ Try turning the needle around and insert the thread through the other side of the needle's eye. During the manufacturing process, the needle's

eye is punched through the needle shank in one direction and this first or "front" side of the eye is larger than the other side. The thread will fit through the front side much more easily.

If all else fails, use a needle threader! There are many different types available, some of which have a very fine threading wire at one end and a coarser wire at the other. If you like using needle threaders, it pays to keep a few on hand in case the wire on one wears out.

Beeswax

EACH TIME a thread is pulled through a quilt sandwich, it becomes a bit worn. It's a good idea to wax quilting thread before you begin to quilt, to retain the original strength of the thread. As you stitch, the wax will wear away a little, leaving the thread still strong. Wax also helps to prevent thread from tangling. For the strongest application, pull the thread through a cake of wax to coat it. Then place it between two sheets of typing paper and press with a warm iron. The wax will penetrate and coat the thread so that it will glide smoothly through the quilt layers without shedding small chunks of wax as you stitch.

Scissors

KEEP A pair of 3"-long embroidery scissors handy for cutting thread. I wear mine on a 36"-long ribbon around my neck while quilting. That way, I never have to search for them when I need them. Another option is to use thread clips. Thread clips have short blades, and some types come with blunt ends, so that you are less likely to slip and snip the fabric while clipping a thread close to the surface of the quilt.

Lamps and Magnifiers

IF YOU have difficulty seeing your stitching, especially if natural light is not available, consider investing in a good portable lamp with a swing arm. Some of the newer quilting frames have a special fitting for attaching this type of portable lamp. Also available is a lamp that hangs from a strap around your neck to aim light directly onto your stitching. True-color lamps that reflect the full spectrum of light can be invaluable for all kinds of sewing and quilting tasks. You can choose from lamps that fit onto a table, desk, or floor frame; table lamps; and floor lamps with swing arms. Also available are true-color bulbs that fit standard lamp fixtures.

Another helpful stitching aid is a large magnifying device. This, too, can be worn around your neck to magnify the area on which you are stitching. Check ads in quilting magazines for sources selling these lamps and magnifiers.

Thimbles

THE BEST thimble for hand quilting depends on the way you like to stitch. Some thimbles have a brass fitting or built-in ridge around the top edge to give extra leverage as you push the needle through the quilt layers. Others have a slightly indented top for pushing with the tip of your finger. This is my preferred thimble for hand quilting and hand piecing.

Some quilters prefer to use the side of their thimbles and choose traditionally shaped thimbles for this method. Others never become accustomed to wearing a traditional metal thimble at all and would rather use a soft leather thimble. Still others like using a metal tailor's thimble with an open end that allows the finger to protrude slightly, enabling the quilter to push a needle with the side of the thimble. Some quilters do not use a thimble at all, but most agree that some kind of finger protection is necessary if you want to avoid extremely sore fingers. If you are one who does not like the feel of any kind of thimble on your finger, try using a ThimblePad. These ¼" suede circles have adhesive on one side. Place the adhesive side on the tip of the finger that pushes a needle and quilt as you normally would. ThimblePads feel almost like you are wearing no thimble at all and they are strong enough to last for a very long time without becoming worn. They are especially effective to wear on your thumb for quilting in any direction.

Marking Tools

WHEN MARKING a quilting pattern onto a quilt top, the marked stitching lines need to be just dark enough to see from "a stitching distance" away. Use a marking method that can be removed easily. Good choices include the following:

LEAD PENCILS

Some quiltmakers feel that a fine, lightly drawn pencil line may be the best way to mark a quilt top. It is important to use a light touch when marking quilting lines. If necessary, it is easy to go back over a line that is too light, but it is very difficult to remove a pencil line that is so dark that the lead is actually embedded in the cotton fibers. I recommend using a size 0.5 mm mechanical pencil with a 2H lead. This is a hard lead, which breaks easily when too much pressure is put on it, so it forces you to mark lightly in order to avoid breaking the lead. In addition, a mechanical pencil never needs sharpening, the width of the line it draws is always the same, and it is similar to the width of the quilting thread. A regular No. 4 pencil has the same hardness of lead, but it loses its sharp point quickly, which means that the lines become thicker the longer you use it. It is easy to disguise a pencil line if the stitches hide all or half of its width, but very difficult to hide if the marked line is wider than the thickness of the thread.

COLORED PENCILS

A variety of white, blue, silver, and yellow marking pencils are available for marking on dark fabrics, where lead pencil marks do not show up. My favorite is the Sanford Prismacolor No. 916 Canary Yellow. This pencil has more wax in its lead than other colored pencils have, so it glides more smoothly and marks more easily on fabric. Caution: The lead in this pencil is so soft that if you press hard, you will leave a permanent line on the fabric. And if you use it on light-colored fabric, the line will be permanent, so take care to use this pencil on only medium- and dark-colored fabrics.

CHALK MARKERS

Chalk markers are also useful for marking on dark fabrics. The powdered, colored chalk is dispensed through a small container with a wheel at its base. A small amount of chalk is released as the wheel rolls across the fabric. It should be noted that colored chalk is sometimes difficult to remove from white and light-colored fabrics.

WATER-SOLUBLE MARKING PENS

These pens are available in a variety of colors, making it possible to mark clearly visible lines on a variety of colors. Instructions for removing the marks after the stitching is complete are included with each pen. It is important to test these pens on your fabric first to make sure you can remove the color. The ink is a chemical that may not react favorably with the fabric and batting combination you have chosen for your quilt.

Sometimes the ink reappears months or years later, either in the original color or as a brownish color. It is also important to note that pressing with an iron over marks made with these pens can set the color, making it impossible to remove. Use these pens with caution, removing the ink as you go rather than waiting until all the quilting is finished. To aid in the removal of the markings, wash the completed quilt in cold water with gentle agitation, allowing it to sit in the water after agitation for 20 minutes. Drain the water from the machine and repeat the process three more times. Then drain the water and spin dry.

SOAP SLIVERS

Soap slivers are also effective for marking on dark fabrics. The soap is easy to remove, but the marking edge dulls fairly quickly.

CORNSTARCH AND CINNAMON

In the past, some quiltmakers liked to use cornstarch or spices to mark quilting designs. You may find the method just as suitable today. This marking method works best on a stationary quilt that is mounted in a frame. Simply brush or blow away the cornstarch or cinnamon when the stitching is finished. To give it a try:

1. Draw the desired quilting design on heavy paper. A brown paper grocery bag is ideal.

2. Using an unthreaded size 90 or 100 needle in your sewing machine, stitch on the traced lines to make perforations in the paper.

3. Place the paper with the perforated design on the quilt top and carefully rub cornstarch through the holes in the paper. When the paper pattern is removed, a trail of cornstarch remains on the

quilt surface, outlining the design. Cornstarch works well on darker colors. For light colors, use cinnamon.

STILETTO OR BLUNT NEEDLE

Another marking method that leaves no colored mark on the quilt surface was used by old-time quiltmakers on all-white, whole-cloth quilts. They used a blunt needle or pointed instrument like a stiletto to mark indentations in the surface of the quilt top. Over time, I have come to prefer this method of marking over any other. It allows you to mark a quilt without leaving permanent marks. However, this type of marking is most visible when a cotton or cotton-blend batting is used in the quilt. I have a quilt that I have been quilting on infrequently for more than a year, and I have found that the marks have remained visible for several months. To use this method:

1. Place a ruler (or quilting template) along the area to be marked.

2. Run a stiletto, a tapestry needle, or the eye end of a quilting needle along the template or ruler, exerting enough pressure to make a visible indentation in the surface of the quilt top.

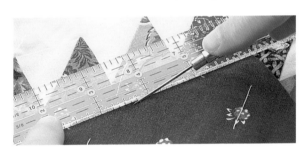

HERA MARKER

A Hera marker is a tool that was originally used in Japan for marking silk fabric without leaving any chemical residue or other marking on the fabric. While many of these markers were originally made of ivory, today a Hera marker is a small, white plastic tool with a curved, sharp edge. It is easy to hold in your hand, and it is great for marking straight lines on quilt tops. Any lines you score with a Hera marker, however, will be almost impossible to remove, so for best results, follow these steps.

1. Position an acrylic ruler on the quilt sandwich at the exact place you want to mark a straight line.

2. Holding the ruler firmly with your left hand, place the curved edge of the Hera marker next to the right edge of the ruler. Pressing down very firmly, begin to move the Hera marker slowly back and forth next to the ruler. Do not lift the Hera marker from the fabric as you score this straight line. You can move and reposition the ruler, if necessary, to extend the line, as long as the Hera stays in place until you are ready to begin marking again.

MASKING TAPE

Masking tape is another alternative for marking straight quilting lines without leaving a visible mark on the quilt top. Tape in widths of ¼", ¾", and 1" are most useful for this marking method.

Place a ruler on the quilt top where you want to quilt a straight line. Place the masking tape next to the ruler on the quilt top. Use ¼"-wide tape when you wish to mark single straight lines or double lines, spaced ¼" apart. The ¾" and 1" widths are good for marking cross-hatching lines.

Use this method in small areas and always remove the tape when you stop quilting. Leaving masking tape in place for long periods of time can leave a sticky residue on your quilt top that will pick up dirt and lint and be difficult to remove. Avoid using old masking tape, as adhesive tends to become gummier with age. I have found that even new masking tape can leave a residue on fabric, so I avoid it for that reason.

Hoops

TODAY WE have a wide choice of hoops available. Use the following guidelines to choose a hoop that will best suit your quilting style.

♦ Choose a hoop size that is large enough so you can quilt for a reasonable length of time without having to reposition it, yet small enough that you can reach to quilt easily in the middle area.

♦ Take into consideration the size of your project and choose an appropriately sized hoop. Round hoops range from small (8") to medium-size (14") and large (18"). Square and oval hoops are also available in different sizes. Of these three types, the square and round hoops put the most even tension on a quilt sandwich; oval hoops are less consistent.

♦ Consider how you like to sit when using a hoop. If you enjoy relaxing on a couch or curling up in a recliner while you stitch, a handheld hoop may be the best choice. If you like to sit in a chair that has firm back support while you quilt, you may prefer using a hoop on a stand that allows you to turn the project in a 360º circle. (For more information about the square hoop on a stand shown here, see "Resources" on page 80.)

GraceHoop2 Quilting Frame

Frames

QUILTING AT a frame offers some advantages that lap quilting and quilting in a hoop do not. Consider the following when determining whether you want to invest in a floor frame.

A floor frame allows you to stretch all three layers of a quilt sandwich throughout the entire quilting process, which eliminates the possibility of distortions or uneven areas that can come from positioning and repositioning a hoop many times. The most time-honored, traditional quilting frames featured four rails on which the three layers of a quilt sandwich were stretched. As the quilting progressed, one rail was rolled up to allow the quilter to reach unquilted areas. (For more information on this frame, see "Resources" on page 80.) I use my four-rail floor frame for basting my quilts prior to quilting.

GraciBee Quilting Frame

Today, many quilting frames offer two-, three-, or four-rail options. Two-rail frames require basting the quilt sandwich together before putting it on the frame, while frames with three or four rails enable you to put a quilt onto the rails without basting the layers together first. The frame shown here has four rails and a system of forty ratchets that allow you to control the tension on the quilt top, batting, and backing individually. If you like to use a rocking motion as you stitch, you may prefer to have less tension on the layers of the quilt sandwich, so that you can move the needle back and forth easily. If you prefer to stab stitch, however, you may prefer to have more tension on the quilt sandwich, because the needle only goes vertically through the three layers as you take each individual stitch. (For more information on this frame, see "Resources" on page 80.)

Another benefit of a floor frame is that it supports the entire weight of the quilt, keeping it away from your body while you stitch. This makes it easier and more enjoyable to quilt a bed-sized quilt, especially in warmer months.

Grace Z44 Quilting Frame

Try It before You Buy It!

Investigate the benefits of as many quilt frames as you can before purchasing one. Schedule a visit to your local quilt shop and try stitching at the frame they display, or stop by manufacturers' booths at regional or national quilt shows. Getting as much information and personal experience as possible will help you make sure that you are investing in the frame that is best for you.

To quilt comfortably at a frame, start by choosing a chair that has firm back support and the capability to adjust the height, so that your spine will stay as straight and relaxed as possible while you quilt. And it's a good idea to use a chair with rollers, so that you can slide back and forth at the frame with a minimum of effort. After you have inserted a quilt into the frame, follow these steps to ensure that you feel the greatest degree of comfort as you stitch.

1. Set the chair in front of the frame, at a comfortable height for your body. Be seated, and check that your legs are at a comfortable distance from the floor and your spine is straight.

2. Place your arms as if you were going to quilt, holding your left arm underneath the quilt sandwich and your right arm on top (reverse if left-handed). Think about how your body feels as you do this. If you find that you are bent over enough that your back feels uncomfortable, the height of the frame is incorrect.

Incorrect Posture

3. Adjust the height of the frame until you are able to sit in a natural position while you quilt, without putting undue pressure on your back. Your legs should feel relaxed and comfortable, and you should be able to stitch for half an hour to an hour without stress.

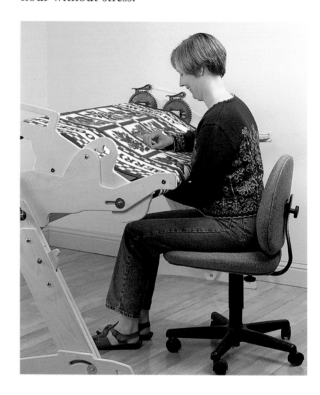

Correct Posture

Listen to the Music!

When you feel comfortable quilting at a floor frame, it can be tempting to quilt for long periods of time without getting up; however, sitting too long without taking a break now and then is not good for your body. Give yourself a foolproof way to ensure that you will take a break at regular intervals. Put on one or two of your favorite CDs and enjoy stitching to music you enjoy. When the last song ends, stop stitching. Get up from the frame and take a five-minute walk, or do a few household tasks. When you feel rejuvenated, you can put on more music and come back to quilting feeling refreshed and energized.

Making Templates and Stencils

AFTER YOU CHOOSE the quilting design(s) you wish to use, you may need templates or stencils to transfer some of the designs to your quilt top. A wide variety of quilting stencils and templates are now available. You can also make your own. Template plastic, X-ray film, and clear plastic are all suitable materials for making quilting templates and stencils. Lightweight cardboard is also an option, although it makes checking for correct design placement more difficult than with see-through materials.

A template may be best for marking a simple, isolated design that will be repeated on your quilt top. Make a stencil for continuous-line designs or for more complex designs that include interior details. To make a template, mark the design on your chosen template material, and cut the outside edges of the template the actual size of the quilting design. To make a stencil, mark the entire design on the template material, but do not cut the outside edges. To cut detail lines inside either a template or a stencil, use a tool designed for cutting out pencil-thin lines. An electric hot pen will allow you to "melt away" the marked detail lines on template plastic; however, be careful not to melt away too much of the plastic or the template may not be usable. A double-bladed X-Acto knife will also cut a pencil-thin line; if you choose this option, be careful to cut very smoothly, so that curved lines of your quilting design will not have points or angles. As with learning any new technique, practice will improve your skill, so work slowly and patiently and don't give up if your first template or stencil is not perfect. Just try again and you'll soon become expert at making your own templates and stencils.

If the quilting design you want to use is complex, such as a floral arrangement with many flowers and leaves in it, use a light box to mark the design directly on your quilt top. Office- and architectural-supply stores usually stock light boxes. You can also make a light box (see section below). To use a light box, mark a master pattern of the design on the plain paper (freezer paper works well for large designs). Tape the master pattern on top of the light box, layer the portion of the quilt top to be marked over the master pattern, and use a gentle touch as you trace the quilting design with the marking tool of your choice. It is a common tendency to mark heavily when using a light box, because you cannot see the line you are marking easily when there is light behind it. To make sure that the lines you are marking are not too dark, occasionally slip a white piece of paper between the light box and quilt top to check.

To make your own light box:

1. Separate your dining-room table as if you were going to add an extra leaf. If your table does not separate, you can use two card tables or end tables of the same height.

2. Place a piece of glass, plastic, or Plexiglas over the opening. You can have a piece of glass custom-cut to fit your table at a glass shop, if desired, and frame or tape the edges to avoid cutting your fingers on the sharp edges. For an added fee, you can have glass edges finished.

3. Position a table lamp on the floor beneath the glass.

Quilting Designs

T HE SHADED area of each cable template indicates a single template you can make to repeat the cable design along a border. Using a photocopy machine, enlarge the design of your choice to a size that will fit your border. If the enlarging process distorts the design, reshape the pattern when tracing it to make your template. Use the notches as placement guides. Note that corners require special attention (see "Cables" on page 15).

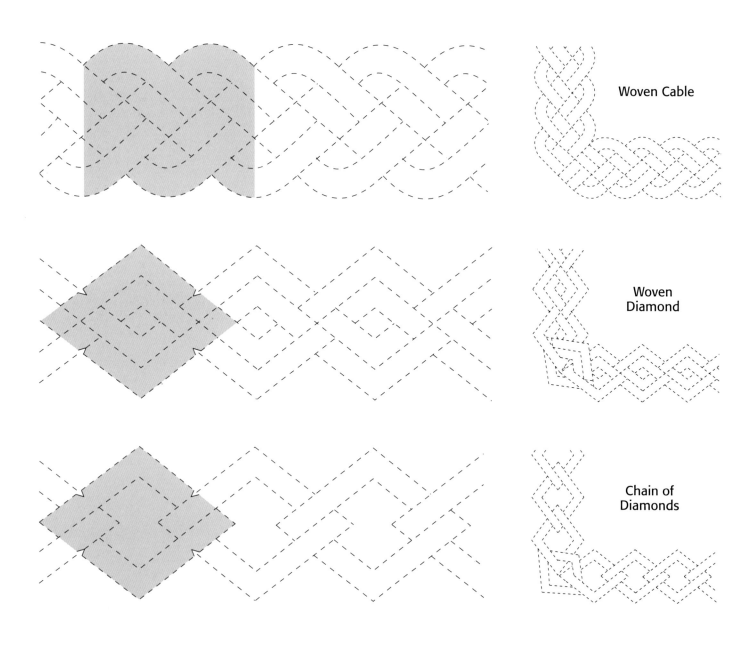

Woven Cable

Woven Diamond

Chain of Diamonds

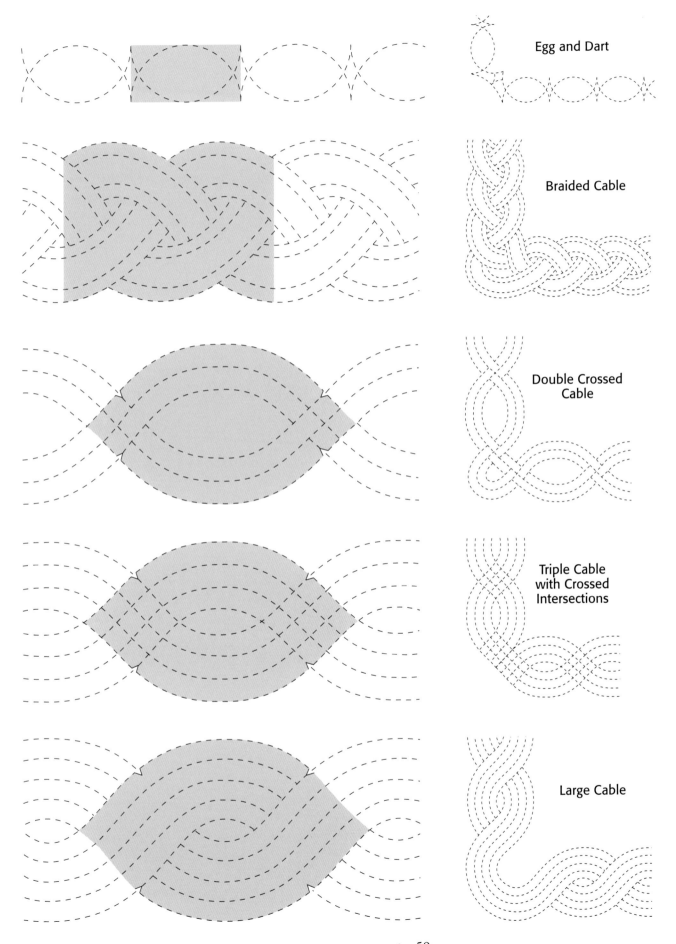

Egg and Dart

Braided Cable

Double Crossed
Cable

Triple Cable
with Crossed
Intersections

Large Cable

Rose

Pineapple

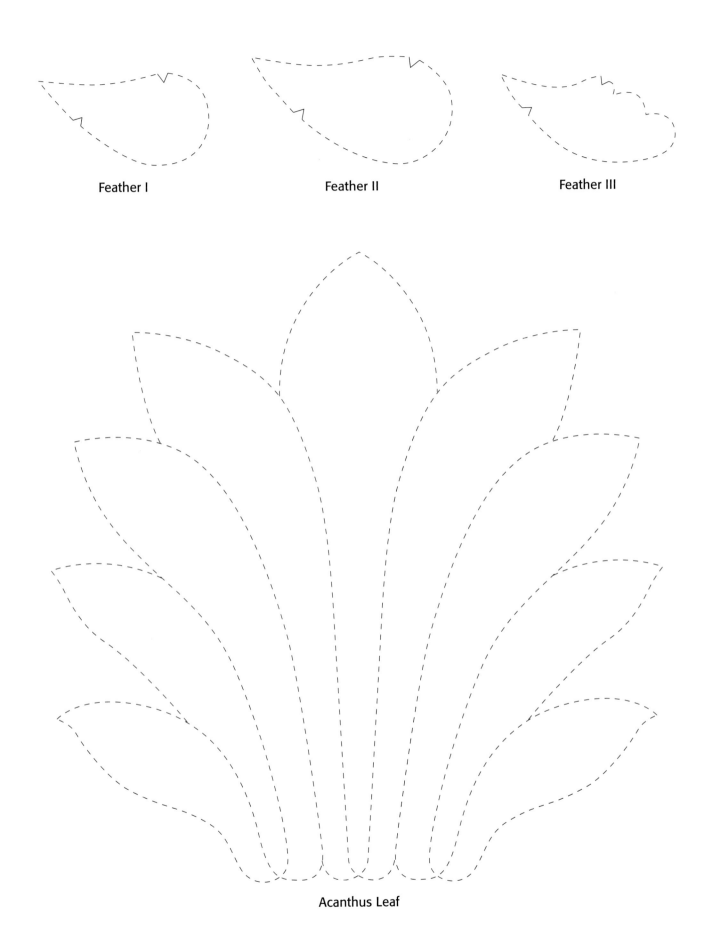

Feather I

Feather II

Feather III

Acanthus Leaf

True Lover's Knot

Preparing the Quilt Top

TO MARK QUILTING designs on a quilt top, use one of the following methods.

♦ Mark all designs before you layer the quilt top. This method allows the quilting process to take place without interruption. If you plan to quilt in a hoop (see pages 74–75), or to lap quilt without a hoop (see pages 73–74), a few of your pre-marked lines may wear off before you finish, requiring you to do some remarking.

♦ Mark the quilting designs as you go. A few of the marking methods described on pages 52–54 can be used only in this way. I prefer to mark as I quilt, because I can use very light marking lines and easily make changes as I stitch.

♦ Before layering the quilt sandwich, use a light box to plan and mark continuous areas, such as border designs, and complex motifs in plain areas. Then mark fill-in designs as your stitching progresses.

After the quilt top is marked, prepare it for quilting as follows.

♦ Clip stray threads, especially if a light fabric is used next to a dark one and dark thread was used to sew the two together. If the thread strays to the light side of the seam, it will cause a shadow, detracting from the clean seam line.

♦ Trim points and seam allowances. Untrimmed points can shadow through your quilt top. If two seam allowances within a given seam are not the same width, trim them even.

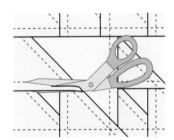

Trim all patchwork seams
to an even width—usually ¼"—
before layering and quilting the top.

Preparing the Backing

KEEPING THESE THINGS in mind when preparing a quilt backing.

Selecting the Fabric

♦ Each side of a quilt should wear at the same rate. Do not sacrifice quality when choosing fabric for a backing.

♦ Choose backing fabric of the same value as the quilt top. A light backing is more appropriate for a white quilt than a dark backing that could show through to the right side. For a dark quilt, a dark backing is appropriate.

♦ Printed fabrics tend to disguise quilting stitches, so if you are a beginning quilter consider a print for the backing.

♦ Match the color of the thread to the patchwork or appliqué pieces so that the quilting stitches are unobtrusive. A printed backing helps to camouflage different colors of thread.

♦ Add a surprise to a quilt backing by piecing together large leftover scraps from the fabrics used to make the quilt top. For this type of backing, remember that you will need to quilt over seams on the back as well as on the front of the quilt.

Piecing the Backing

FOLLOW THESE steps to piece backing of the size you need.

1. Remove the selvages and preshrink the backing fabric by washing and drying it.

2. Press the fabric; fold lines and major wrinkles will not "ease out" with quilting.

3. For a backing with one seam, press the seam open. Center the batting and quilt top over the seam. Trim the batting and backing to 3" or 4" from the edges of the quilt top on all sides.

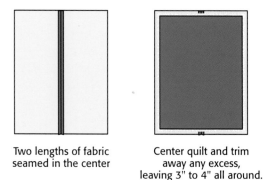

Two lengths of fabric seamed in the center

Center quilt and trim away any excess, leaving 3" to 4" all around.

To assemble the backing in three sections, use one full width of fabric and split the second width down the center. Sew the lengths together and press the seams open. Center the backing on the quilt top and trim the edges as described above.

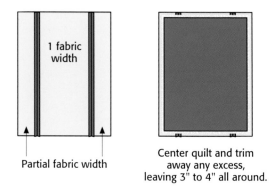

1 fabric width

Partial fabric width

Center quilt and trim away any excess, leaving 3" to 4" all around.

Choosing the Batting

PAST GENERATIONS OF quilters had only two choices for batting—cotton or wool. Cotton batting required careful carding and cleaning to remove the tiny, hard cotton seeds. Wool batting required extensive cleaning to remove the dirt and animal oils. Today, no such labor is required for batting preparation, but it is important to know about the many types now available and the effects they will have on a finished quilt. Since there are so many different manufacturers and each one makes several different batting products, the choices can be confusing. Every quiltmaker will have different criteria for her choice of batting. Read through the following discussion of batting types and experiment until you find the particular brand and type you like best.

Cotton Batting

DURING A visit to the Virginia Quilt Museum in Harrisonburg, Virginia, in the fall of 2002, I saw an antique appliqué displayed beside a newly made appliqué quilt. Seeing these two quilts so close to each other made it obvious that their soft drape and overall look were virtually identical. Even though one quilt had been made over a century before the other, they could have been made at the same time. The reason for this similarity was in the way they hung and their soft, quilted appearance. Both quilts contained 100% cotton batting. This common element gave them the same soft, tactile quality. The quilting stitches seated softly into the cotton fibers, creating beautiful light and shadow in the surface texture of both quilts.

I believe that cotton batting is the best choice for hand quilting for several reasons. Even if the look and feel of cotton are discounted, cotton is cool in summer because the natural fibers are able to "breathe"; and it is warm in winter due to the density of the fibers. Cotton stands the test of time, and best of all, it is easy to needle. If you enjoy the hand-quilting process, you will probably like this type of batting.

MOUNTAIN MIST BLUE RIBBON

A question I can be sure I will be asked at any gathering where my quilts are shown is, "What kind of batting do you use?" My answer is always the same: "My favorite batting is Mountain Mist Blue Ribbon cotton, split to create a fine, thin layer." This batting is made with a card-and-bond process that opens up the long cotton fibers. Then layers of these cotton fibers are built on top of each other to create the batting. A Glazene finish made of acrylic resin is added to both sides to stabilize the cotton fibers. This finish will not wash away when a finished quilt is laundered, which means that you can space your quilting stitches up to 2½" apart without fear that the batting will migrate. There is minimal shrinkage, so there is no prewashing.

All elements of a quilt need to be proportional. If the pieces in the quilt top are small and the overall dimensions of the quilt are small, then the quilting lines should be spaced close together, the quilting stitches should be short, and the batting should be thin. Batting that is too thick will cause a wall quilt to hang poorly.

You can split the Mountain Mist Blue Ribbon batting by removing the Glazene finish from one side. The Glazene finish feels similar to very thin tissue paper. Lay your quilt backing, wrong side up, on a flat surface and position the batting on top of the backing. Starting at one corner, lift up the Glazene finish and gently peel it away from the cotton fibers underneath. It will come up easily, leaving behind a ⅛"-thick layer of cotton batting. Discard the Glazene finish when you have removed it from the batting. (Very few of the cotton fibers will remain adhered to it, so it is too thin to use as a batting layer by itself.)

Place your quilt top on top of the batting and baste the three layers together with thread if you are planning to quilt in a hoop or on your lap. When using cotton batting, the basting stitches can be large and placed 4" to 5" apart. Close basting is unnecessary, as the cotton batting acts like flannel, adhering to the layers of cotton fabric above and below it.

Because the Glazene finish has been removed from one side of the batting, you will need to space your quilting lines at ¼" to ½" intervals in order to stabilize the cotton fibers in your finished quilt. If you are a beginning quilter, you will find it easy to quilt 8 to 10 stitches per inch on this batting. If you are a more experienced quilter, you may enjoy quilting 12 to 14 stitches per inch.

FAIRFIELD SOFT TOUCH COTTON

Fairfield Soft Touch Cotton batting is needlepunched and has a ⅛" loft, which makes it appropriate for creating the flat look of an antique quilt. There is minimal shrinkage and no prewashing is necessary. Quilting lines can be spaced 2" to 4" apart. Because of the low loft, you can quilt anywhere from 8 up to 12 or 14 stitches per inch.

MOUNTAIN MIST NATURAL COTTON

Mountain Mist Natural Cotton batting is another excellent choice for hand quilting. I use this batting on bed-sized quilts. Once again, it is due to proportion. A larger quilt can benefit from a more substantial bat-

ting. There is minimal shrinkage and no prewashing needed. This bleached, 100% cotton batting is made the same way as Mountain Mist Blue Ribbon, but it features a natural starch finish rather than Glazene acrylic resin. Because natural starch will wash away the first time a quilt is laundered, you will need to space your quilting lines very close together; ½" to 1" intervals are best. You can quilt 8 to 10 stitches per inch with this batting.

QUILTER'S DREAM COTTON

Quilter's Dream Cotton batting has no scrim or binders. The fibers are laid flat and combed, so that they cross over each other in many places, creating a consistently smooth surface. It is also needlepunched, which means that the batting is passed through a series of needles that move up and down, locking the fibers in place. There is 3% shrinkage and no need for prewashing. Quilter's Dream Cotton Request batting has a very thin loft, while Quilter's Dream Cotton Select is a midloft batting. Both are appropriate for hand quilting and easy to needle. Quilting lines may be spaced up to 8" apart. You can quilt 10 to 12 stitches per inch on Request and 8 to 10 stitches per inch on Select.

Polyester Batting

MANY QUILTMAKERS do not enjoy quilting through a cotton batting because the cotton fibers are compact and require more force to manipulate the needle through the layers. This makes polyester batting an attractive choice for hand quilting. Polyester is nonallergenic, resilient, and lightweight. However, it differs from cotton in several ways. First, polyester fibers tend to "beard," creating fuzzy, whitish areas on a finished quilt. Some brands are worse than others. If the polyester fibers are heat bonded rather than chemically bonded, the batting is less prone to bearding. Check the packaging for the bonding method used. Second, polyester batting may not stand the test of time as well as cotton batting. Years ago, my mother made a quilt for my husband and me that contained an extra-thick polyester batting. The quilt was nice and fluffy, and we used it in our bedroom. Through normal wear over the next 10 years, the quilt became flatter and flatter until it looked as though there were no batting inside it at all. If you are making a bed quilt that will be laundered frequently and receive a great deal of wear, you may wish to consider cotton batting.

MOUNTAIN MIST QUILT LIGHT

Mountain Mist Quilt Light batting is lightweight and has a low loft, which makes it a good choice for simulating the look of an antique quilt. It is also a nice choice for quilted wearables. There is no shrinkage with this type of batting. It is easy to needle and you can easily quilt anywhere from 8 up to 16 stitches per inch. Quilting lines can be spaced as far as 3" to 4" apart.

FAIRFIELD TRADITIONAL

If you prefer a fuller or puffier look to your quilt, standard-weight polyester batting is the best choice. Fairfield Traditional batting is needlepunched, which means that the fibers pass through a series of barbed needles that move up and down, locking the fibers together. This process gives the batting a dense, even consistency. There is no need for prewashing this batting, but it is a good idea to lay the batting flat for 24 hours before layering it in a quilt sandwich. Quilting lines can be spaced 2" to 4" apart, and you can quilt 8 to 10 stitches per inch with this batting.

Cotton-Polyester Batting

WHEN COTTON and polyester fibers are blended, the result is batting that features the desirable characteristics of each fiber. Cotton-polyester batting is both lightweight and easy to needle, like polyester. It has a lower loft that is more like cotton batting. The cotton fibers also help to make this type of batting cooler in summer and warmer in winter than 100% polyester.

MOUNTAIN MIST GOLD

The mixture of 50% cotton and 50% polyester fibers in this batting makes it easier to needle than 100% cotton. There is less than 1% shrinkage and no prewashing is necessary. It has a fairly low loft. You can start out quilting 8 to 10 stitches per inch and move up to 12 to 14 stitches per inch if desired.

FAIRFIELD COTTON CLASSIC

Fairfield Cotton Classic is 80% cotton and 20% polyester. It has a bonded surface finish with a slight resin that stabilizes the fibers. It has less than ¼" loft and is not suitable for splitting. There is no need for prewashing, but it is a good idea to open up the package and lay the batting flat for 24 hours before layering it

in a quilt sandwich. Quilting lines should be spaced at 2" to 4" intervals. You can quilt 8 to 10 stitches per inch with this batting.

Other Batting Options

WHILE COTTON and polyester batting are most commonly used for hand quilting, there are other options available. Consider the characteristics of these types of batting and decide whether they would be suitable for the type of quilt you wish to make.

♦ Silk is a natural fiber that is very fine, extremely lightweight, and easy to quilt. However, it is very expensive and much more difficult to locate than other types of batting. Silk batting is desirable in clothing because it offers texture and warmth without added weight. Check ads in quilting magazines for sources and availability of silk batting.

♦ Wool is another natural fiber that is very easy to needle. It provides warmth and a soft look like cotton batting. However, it has a tendency to beard like polyester batting. If you choose to use wool batting, enclose it in a cheesecloth casing to keep bearding to a minimum.

♦ Comforter batting manufacturers produce a thicker polyester batting that is suitable for creating the fuller look of a comforter. These quilts are usually tied rather than quilted. The ties or tacks can be placed at 4" intervals on comforter-weight batting, which makes tying a speedy alternative to hand quilting.

♦ Polyester fleece, available by the yard, is a smooth batting that is flatter than cotton, but its density makes it difficult to achieve tiny quilting stitches.

♦ Cotton flannel has virtually no loft and is not as easy to quilt through as cotton batting. This would be a good choice for stabilizing a wool quilt, since wool has a tendency to stretch out of shape.

♦ For a dark quilt, it may be a good idea to use a dark batting if you are using a polyester batting so that there will be no risk of white batting bearding through either side of the quilt.

Layering and Basting

FOR ANY QUILTING method that requires basting layers together before the quilting process begins, follow these steps.

1. Place the prepared backing, right side down, on a large, flat work surface or quilt frame, smoothing out wrinkles. Secure the backing to the surface with masking tape, or to the frame with tacks, to keep it smooth, taut, and straight, with all four corners at 90° angles.

2. Smooth the quilt batting on top of the backing.

3. Lay the quilt top, right side up, on top of the batting, centering it. Pin all three layers together at 6" to 8" intervals around the outside edge, making sure that there are no wrinkles in any of the layers and that the top is smooth and flat.

4. Baste the layers together with long stitches, using a 3"- to 4"-long needle. For more information on ordering these needles, see "Resources" on page 80. Space the basting stitches 2" apart across the width and length of the quilt top. I recommend basting with thread only, rather than with safety pins or plastic tacks, which can leave holes.

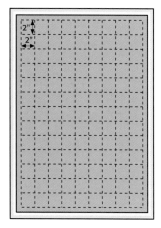

Baste the layers together
with a 3"- to 4"-long needle.

5. Remove the basted quilt sandwich from the work surface or frame. Fold the excess backing and batting onto the quilt top and baste in place to create a temporary binding. The temporary binding will prevent edges from fraying as you quilt.

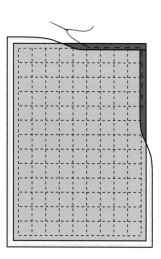

Have a Basting Party!

I like to lap quilt without a hoop, so whenever I baste a large quilt, I stretch the layers on a full-size, four-pole traditional frame and invite my quilting friends to a basting party. In a few hours, the entire quilt is basted and I serve lunch as a thank-you, knowing full well that my guests will invite me to return the favor. If you do not own a full-size frame, borrow one from a friend or fellow guild member, or better yet, encourage your guild to invest in a full-size frame to loan or rent out for basting parties.

Hand Quilting

THE GOAL OF hand quilting is to create a pattern of even stitches that enhance the beauty of a patchwork or appliqué quilt. Whether you are new to hand quilting or already an experienced stitcher, the following pages will put effective techniques and helpful tricks at your fingertips.

Hand-Quilting Standards

THE HALLMARK of beautiful hand quilting is short, evenly spaced stitches. When you first begin hand quilting, however, it's more important to concentrate on making stitches that follow the quilting design without "wobbling" off the marked line. Good quilting stitches are also evenly spaced; that is, the length of the stitch is the same as the length of the space between stitches. Short stitches will come with practice as you become more comfortable with the process and develop your own stitching rhythm.

equally beautiful on the front and back of your quilt. Master quilters make such even stitches that it's impossible to distinguish the back from the front of a whole-cloth quilt.

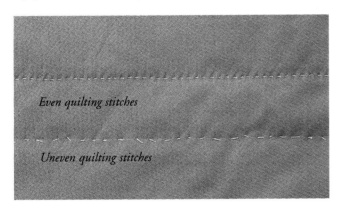

Even quilting stitches

Uneven quilting stitches

One way to measure your quilting progress is to count your stitches. Place a ruler on the quilt top along a quilted line and count the stitches in an inch. Seven to nine stitches per inch is the standard for good-quality quilting. Excellent quilting has 9 to 12 stitches per inch. Any more than that per inch is exceptional! With lots of practice, your quilting stitches will be

Coat Thread with Beeswax

Instead of running each individual strand of thread you use through a cake of beeswax, try this trick for coating the whole spool of thread at once. Cover a 3" x 18" piece of cardboard or Masonite with muslin, making sure that both sides are encased in the fabric. Wind an entire spool of quilting thread lengthwise around the muslin-covered rectangle. Rub beeswax over the wound thread, taking care to cover all of it with wax. Place tissue paper over the waxed thread. Using a dry iron set on low heat, iron carefully over all of the wound thread, allowing the beeswax to penetrate the fibers. When the thread is cool, cut through it at both ends of the rectangle, and you'll have an entire spool's worth of 18"-long threads that are ready for quilting.

Threading a Needle

FOLLOW THESE steps to thread a needle easily and quickly. Reverse the hand positions if you are left-handed.

1. Cut the thread to your desired length.

2. Hold the end of the quilting thread between your thumb and index finger of your left hand, so that only a tiny bit of the end is visible.

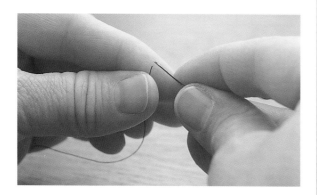

3. Lower the eye of the needle between your fingers, so that it slips easily onto the end of the thread. Pull the thread through, leaving a short tail.

Thread Multiple Needles

To save time and frustration, consider threading as many as 10 needles at a time before you start a quilting session. And check your local quilt shop for needle caddies that hold up to 10 or more threaded needles at a time.

Making a Quilter's Knot

FOLLOW THESE steps to make a quilter's knot that is small and easy to pop through fabric.

1. Hold the threaded needle between the thumb and forefinger of your right hand. Holding the thread tail in your left hand, point the needle toward the thread tail.

2. Grasp the thread tail with your fingers holding the needle. With your left hand, wrap the thread around the needle two or three times.

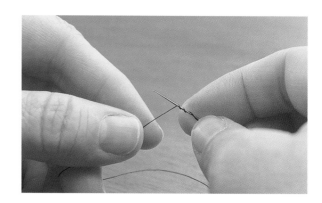

3. Holding the wrapped threads tightly with the right thumb and forefinger, pull the needle all the way through with your left hand. This will result in a small, firm knot at the end of the thread. Don't be concerned if there is a bit of a tail beyond the knot; simply cut it close to the knot.

Starting a Thread

FOLLOW THESE steps to pop a quilter's knot through the quilt top, so that it lodges in the batting layer.

1. Insert the needle into the quilt top approximately ½" ahead of where you wish to begin stitching. Push the needle point between the quilt top and batting and bring it out where you wish to begin quilting. Pull the thread until the knot lies at the surface of the fabric.

2. Give a gentle tug on the thread to pop the knot below the surface of the quilt top. If the knot pops down and then back out again, start over, this time aiming the needle deeper into the batting, allowing the knot to become entangled in the fibers. Then tug more gently to pop the knot inside.

Swishing

If a tail of thread protrudes on the surface after popping the knot, insert the needle between the quilt layers and rotate it toward and past the tail to catch and pull it between the layers. I call this "swishing."

3. Stitch on the marked quilting line, using one of the quilting methods described on pages 73–78.

Ending a Thread

WHEN YOU reach the end of a thread or the end of a stitching line, tie off the thread with a colonial knot. This is an elongated knot that is easier to pull through the quilt layers than a rounder, heavier knot.

To make a colonial knot, follow these steps.

1. Pull the thread taut toward your body with your left hand.

2. Point the threaded needle toward the quilt top, keeping it parallel to the thread. As a way to remember this position, visualize the number 11; the thread with the needle beside it forms an 11.

3. Angle the needle over the top of the thread and wrap it once around the needle point. The thread remains stationary during this process.

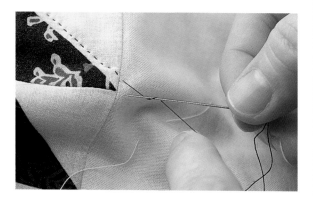

4. Use your free left hand to wrap the thread around the needle point. This will put two wraps of thread around the needle.

5. Reinsert the needle point into the same hole. Then run the needle through the batting layer for about ½" and pull it through until the knot is lying on the quilt surface where the needle and thread entered.

6. Tug the thread, and the knot will pop into the batting. Pull the thread taut and hold your scissors perpendicular to and ⅛" away from the fabric. Clip the thread and use the needle to "swish" the tail into the batting as described on page 71.

The Quilting Stitch

THE QUILTING stitch is a short, evenly spaced running stitch, which is made through all three layers of a quilt to hold them together and to add visual depth to the surface of the finished quilt. Try the following hand-quilting techniques and decide which works best for you.

LAP QUILTING

Quilting without a frame or hoop is popular with many quilters, because the work is portable and it is easy to quilt in a variety of positions—on the floor, at a table, in an easy chair, or in a car. Many people also think lap quilting makes it easier to take small stitches. However, when not stretched taut, the layers can shift, resulting in permanently stitched-in wrinkles on the back of the quilt. On the other hand, if you are experienced at hand sewing, you might find this method the best suited to your stitching style and skill level.

One of the major pitfalls in lap quilting is the tendency to smooth out the backing fabric more than the fabric in the quilt top. To avoid this, as you smooth the backing, be aware that there should be fullness on the backing as well as on the top.

1. Layer and baste the quilt sandwich as shown on page 68.

2. Place one hand underneath the basted quilt and the other on top, smoothing the front and back surfaces so there are no wrinkles. Repeat this process every time you begin a new line of stitching. To ease in any fullness you find or to prevent it from developing while you stitch, place a few straight pins through the layers across the line about to be quilted. The pins are, in essence, a substitute for the quilting frame or hoop that

holds the layers together. It is not necessary to pin on every line of stitching; place pins only where there are not yet any other lines of quilting to help stabilize the layers. Don't neglect this pinning process; it is a necessary supplement to the basting that is already in place.

3. With your nonsewing hand, grasp the quilt in the area you want to stitch, keeping your thumb on top and your other four fingers underneath. Hold a quilt this way when working on a small quilt or when working near the outer edges of any size quilt. When working in center areas, hold your thumb underneath the quilt with the other four fingers, and use it to grasp a handful of the quilt sandwich.

4. The way you grasp the needle as you insert it is different than for traditional stitching methods. Instead of holding your quilting hand on top or above the needle, hold your hand underneath the needle (similar to the way you would in tossing a dart). This hand position minimizes the full arm action needed to take each stitch, and it gives you better leverage as you move the needle in and out of the fabric. It also increases your stitching speed.

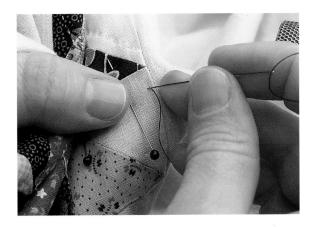

5. As the needle pierces through to the back side of the quilt, move your fingers underneath out of the way to avoid being pricked. Half of the length of the needle should be pushed through to the quilt back. Holding the needle horizontally, pull it back toward the first stitch, dragging the needle point along the backing fabric and following the "backing up" with your fingers underneath the quilt. When the needle reaches the spot where you want it to come back up through the quilt top, push the needle point with your fingers underneath and thumb on top. At the same time, use your fingers that are on top and holding the needle to pull the needle upward. Strive to make the needle come vertically through the layers, to ensure that your stitches will be evenly spaced. This forward-and-back motion of pushing the needle too far and then backing up to make the stitch creates a channel in the batting that allows you to load multiple stitches evenly onto the needle.

6. To make the next stitch, repeat step 5, putting as many stitches on the needle as is comfortable for you before pushing needle and thread through with the thimble on your middle finger.

"ROCKER" QUILTING

The stitching method most commonly used for quilting in a hoop or at a frame is called "rocker" quilting. To stitch this way, the quilt layers must be held taut and smooth while you use a rocking motion to guide the needle through the layers. A short Between needle may be easier to manipulate with this method; however, a longer needle is shown in the following photos for better visibility. To rocker quilt, follow these steps:

1. Stretch the quilt sandwich taut in a frame or hoop.

2. Work with your quilting hand on top and your other hand beneath the quilt. Use the thumb and index finger of your quilting hand to place the needle in the correct position to take the first stitch, holding your middle finger with the thimble at the eye of the needle. (The needle's eye will rest in one of the dimples in the top of the thimble after you have begun the first stitch.)

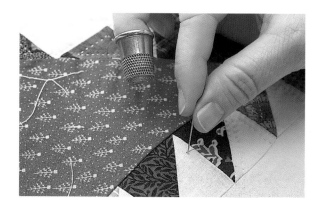

3. Insert the needle through the layers of the quilt sandwich, letting go of it with your thumb and index finger, and use the thimble to push and guide it through the layers in a "rocking" motion.

4. As soon as you feel the needle point coming through to the back side of the quilt sandwich, release the pressure on the thimble. Use your underneath finger to guide the needle back up to the top of the quilt sandwich, reapplying pressure to the thimble to help force the needle back up through the layers. At the same time, use the thumb of your quilting hand to apply downward pressure on the top of the quilt to help force the needle to come up as vertically as possible through the layers.

5. When the point of the needle comes back up through the quilt sandwich, use the thimble to push the needle forward a stitch length. Then apply downward pressure with the thimble to push the needle underneath the quilt sandwich, setting up the "rocking" motion again to take sev-

eral stitches before pulling the needle all the way through the quilt layers.

Make a Liquid Thimble

For protecting the finger you hold underneath a quilt hoop or frame, try using Krazy Glue gel. Carefully put a few drops of the gel on the area of the finger you use to feel the tip of the needle, and use a hairdryer to dry the gel (at least five minutes) until it takes on a whitish-gray color with a matte finish. To add even more protection, you can apply a second layer of gel and dry it in the same way. When used on a noninjured finger, the hard surface of the dried Krazy Glue gel will protect your finger just like a callus. When you finish quilting, you can remove it with acetone or nail-polish remover. *Caution:* If you have sensitive skin or if you are unsure whether the chemicals in Krazy Glue gel will cause you any problems, consult a doctor before using this product.

KNOTLESS QUILTING

Quilting without knots has several advantages. First, it eliminates the need to pop a knot through the fabric of a quilt top each time you begin or end a strand of thread. You will never need to worry about a knot breaking right at the surface of the quilt top or having to undo several inches of quilting and start over again. And because knotless quilting is done with a strand of thread that is twice as long as you would normally use for quilting, you will never have to *start* a thread again; all you will ever need to do is *end* each thread. Finally, there is more flexibility in the finished quilt because there are no knots that can pop through if someone sits on the finished quilt. Follow these steps to try knotless quilting:

1. Hold the end of the quilting thread between your right thumb and index finger. With your left hand, pull the thread down until it reaches your elbow.

2. Fold the thread in half to double this length and cut the thread at that point. Coat the thread with beeswax if desired.

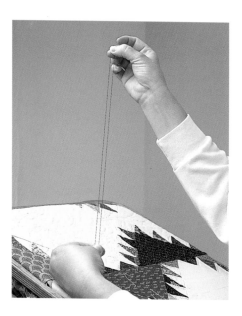

3. Thread a needle you like to use for quilting. Insert the needle into the quilt sandwich wherever you want to begin quilting. Draw the thread only halfway through, allowing the second half of the thread to remain free on the quilt top. Begin quilting and continue stitching until approximately 3" or 4" of thread is left.

4. To end this thread, insert the needle through the quilt top and into the batting. Gently weave the needle back through the previous four or five stitches. Bring the needle up through the quilt top again and clip the thread close to the surface.

5. Thread the needle with the remaining half of the thread and repeat steps 3 and 4. Continue quilting in the same manner throughout the entire quilt.

Show Me!

To demonstrate how secure knotless quilting actually is, try experimenting with it on a small scrap of quilt sandwich before you begin using this method on an actual quilt. Do several inches of quilting with the first half of your thread, ending it as described in step 3 above. Tug on the remaining half of thread to see that your quilting stitches will not come out, even if you pull quite hard on the thread.

QUILTING IN ANY DIRECTION

If you enjoy quilting in a hoop or at a frame, it can be very helpful to know how to quilt in any direction without moving the quilt sandwich. All it takes is your thumb, which is your strongest finger, and a thimble that fits your thumb well. I recommend either a tailor's thimble with dimples all the way around and an open end, or a self-adhesive, ¼" suede ThimblePad. Choose the thimble you like best and follow these steps to learn how to stitch in any direction with ease:

1. To quilt diagonally from lower right to upper left, bring up the thread wherever you wish to start stitching. Use your fingers to insert the needle vertically in position to take the first stitch and feel the needle come through to the back side with a finger of your nonquilting hand.

2. As soon as you feel the point of the needle underneath the quilt sandwich, use your thumb on top to lower the needle so that it comes back up to the right side again, as vertically as possible. Let the needle come out of the fabric for the length of one stitch.

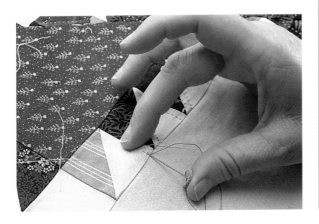

3. Use your thumb to bring the needle back into a vertical position and insert the needle through the quilt sandwich again.

4. Repeat steps 1–3 to stitch a diagonal line.

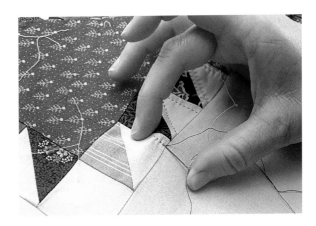

5. To quilt a diagonal line in the opposite direction, simply use your thumb to guide the needle in that direction.

6. To quilt a straight line from left to right, let the strength of your thumb guide the needle toward your right forefinger as you take each stitch.

STAB STITCHING

The alternative stitching method for quilting at a frame is stab stitching. It takes more time than lap quilting and rocker quilting, because each stitch is taken individually. In addition, it can be difficult to make the stitches on the back side of the quilt as even and straight as those on the front. It takes a lot of control and coordination with the hand underneath the quilt to make beautiful quilting stitches with this technique, but it creates less stress on your wrists than the other types of quilting, because the needle is always held vertically. Experiment with this method to see if you like it.

1. Take the first stitch by inserting or "stabbing" the needle vertically through the layers of the quilt sandwich; use your underneath hand to pull the needle all the way through.

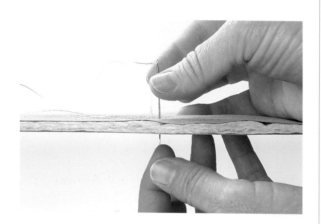

2. Guide the needle vertically up through the top again to complete the first stitch and bring the thread into position to take the next stitch. Continue stitching in the same manner.

Removing Blood Stains

If you prick your finger while quilting and a drop of blood seeps into the fabric, try this trick. Pour a little bit of hydrogen peroxide into a small bowl or cup and insert a cotton swab into the liquid. Gently rub the dampened cotton swab over the stained area and watch the blood disappear as if by magic.

Notes

1. Patsy and Myron Orlofsky, *Quilts in America,* 1–2.
2. Dorothy Osler, *Traditional British Quilts,* 82.
3. Ibid.
4. Rosemary E. Allan, *North Country Quilts and Coverlets from Beamish Museum,* 8.
5. Dorothy Osler, *Traditional British Quilts,* 83.
6. Orlofsky, *Quilts in America,* 136.
7. Osler, *Traditional British Quilts,* 118.
8. Ruth E. Finley, *Old Patchwork Quilts and the Women Who Made Them,* 118.
9. Janet Rae, *The Quilts of the British Isles,* 20.
10. Finley, *Old Patchwork Quilts,* 132.
11. Ibid, 138–139.
12. Orlofsky, *Quilts in America,* 146.
13. Ibid.
14. Allan, *North Country Quilts and Coverlets,* 18.
15. Finley, *Old Patchwork Quilts,* 146.
16. Ibid., 142.
17. Ibid., 140–41.
18. Osler, *Traditional British Quilts,* 20.

Bibliography

Allan, Rosemary E. *North Country Quilts and Coverlets from Beamish Museum County Durham.* Stanley, County Durham, England: Beamish North of England Open Air Museum, 1987.

Colby, Averil. *Patchwork.* London: B.T. Batsford, 1958.

Finley, Ruth E. *Old Patchwork Quilts and the Women Who Made Them.* Newton Center, Mass.: Charles T. Branford Company, 1929.

Hall, Carrie A., and Rose G. Kretsinger, *The Romance of the Patchwork Quilt in America.* New York: Bonanza Books, 1935.

Hall, Eliza Calvert. *Aunt Jane of Kentucky.* Boston: Little, Brown and Company, 1907.

Kimball, Jeana. *Appliqué Borders: An Added Grace.* Bothell, Wash.: That Patchwork Place, 1991.

Kimball, Jeana. *Reflections of Baltimore.* Bothell, Wash.: That Patchwork Place, 1989.

Orlofsky, Patsy and Myron. *Quilts in America.* New York: McGraw-Hill Book Company, 1974.

Osler, Dorothy. *Quilting.* London: Merehurst Limited, 1991.

Osler, Dorothy. *Traditional British Quilts.* London: B.T. Batsford Ltd., 1987.

Rae, Janet. *The Quilts of the British Isles.* New York: E. P. Dutton, 1987.

Resources

StenSource International, Inc.
Phone: 209-536-1148
Web site: www.StenSource.com
Stencils for quilting and painting; sun-face quilting design on page 23

Fairfield Processing
Web site: www.poly-fil.com
Batting

The Grace Company
PO Box 27823
Salt Lake City, UT 84127
Toll-free: 800-264-0644
Frames and hoops

Jeana Kimball's Foxglove Cottage
PO Box 698
Santa Clara, UT 84765
Phone: 435-656-2071
Email: foxglovecottage@ifox.com
Full line of needles for hand quilting

Ott-Lite Technology
Environmental Lighting Company
PO Box 172425
Tampa, FL 33672-0425
Toll-free: 800-842-8848
True-color lamps and magnifying lamps

Quilter's Dream Cotton
589 Central Dr.
Virginia Beach, VA 23454
Toll-free: 888-268-8994
Fax: 800-626-8866
Batting

Sewing Notions, Inc.
PO Box 980707
Ypsilanti, MI 49198
Toll-free: 800-334-4241
ThimblePads

Stearns Technical Textiles Company
Mountain Mist Batting
100 Williams St.
Cincinnati, OH 45215
Toll-free: 800-345-7150
Batting

About the Author

JEANA KIMBALL first learned about needlework from her mother and grandmother, who taught her skills they had learned from their mothers and grandmothers. This shared knowledge links Jeana to six generations of her family, from the late eighteenth century to the present. Jeana places great value on this legacy as she pursues a career in quiltmaking and continues to increase her knowledge and abilities.

Jeana is best known for her appliqué design work, which combines classic elements from the past with contemporary themes. She is the author of numerous appliqué design and pattern books. In her books she often teaches about nineteenth-century women and the tradition of needlework in their lives. Quiltmakers have enjoyed Jeana's work for nearly fifteen years in published works including *Reflections of Baltimore* and *Red and Green: An Appliqué Tradition*.

Living in a small town in southern Utah, Jeana and her husband, Charlie, are the parents of a son and a daughter and the grandparents of three granddaughters, with whom Jeana will share her love of hand quilting.